BRAIN POWER

THE CONSCIOUS AND UNCONSCIOUS BRAIN

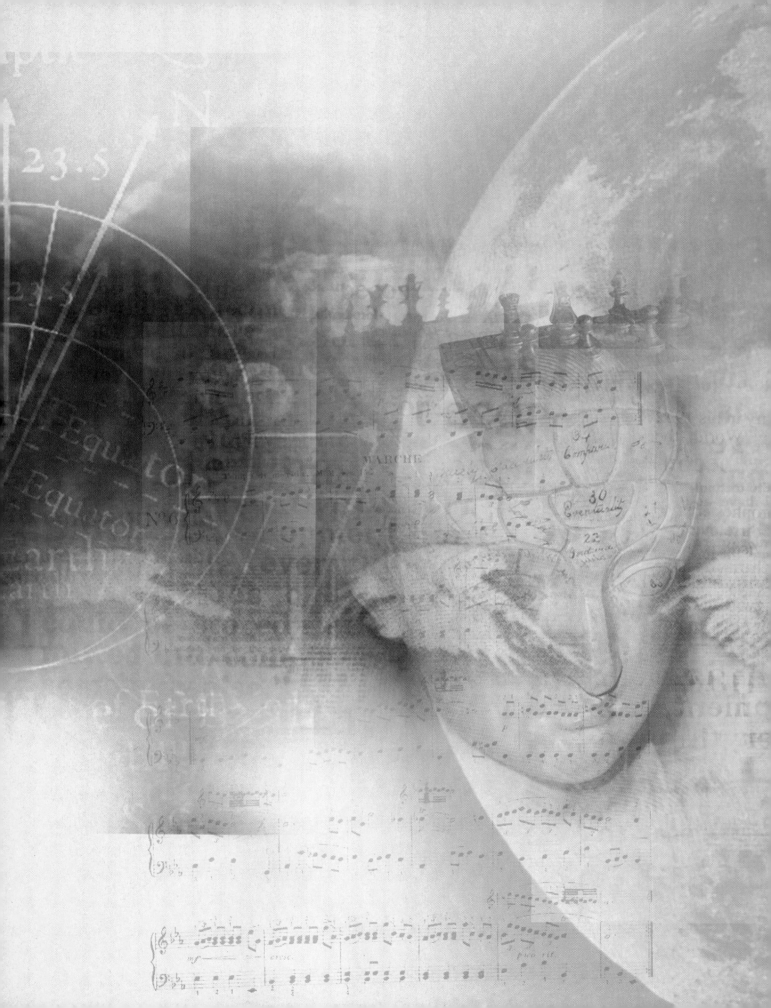

BRAIN POWER

THE CONSCIOUS AND UNCONSCIOUS BRAIN

THE READER'S DIGEST ASSOCIATION LIMITED   LONDON • NEW YORK • SYDNEY • MONTREAL

CONTENTS

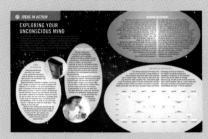

**The Conscious and
Unconscious Brain**
was created and produced
for Reader's Digest, London,
by Duncan Baird Publishers Ltd
Sixth Floor, Castle House
75–76 Wells Street
London W1T 3QH

Managing Editor
Susan Watt

Managing Art Editor
Phil Gilderdale

Text Editors
Marek Walisiewicz, Susan Watt

Designers
Gail Jones, Sheilagh Noble,
Chris Walker

Picture Researcher
Ellen Root

Editorial Assistant
Kelly Bishop

Academic Consultants
Zoltan Dienes, D.Phil.
Reader in Experimental Psychology
University of Sussex

Professor Nicholas Humphrey, Ph.D.
Centre for Philosophy of Natural and Social Science
London School of Economics

CONTRIBUTORS
Sarah Angliss
Nigel C. Benson
Dr. Peter Bull
Jerome Burne
Rita Carter
Professor David Fontana
Dr. Les Lancaster
John McCrone
Dr. Rowland Stout
Marek Walisiewicz

ADDITIONAL THANKS
Tim Foster, Nicola Hodgson,
Marnie Searchwell

For the Reader's Digest
Series Editor Christine Noble
Art Editor Louise Turpin
Editorial Assistant Lucy Murray

Reader's Digest General Books
Editorial Director Cortina Butler
Art Director Nick Clark

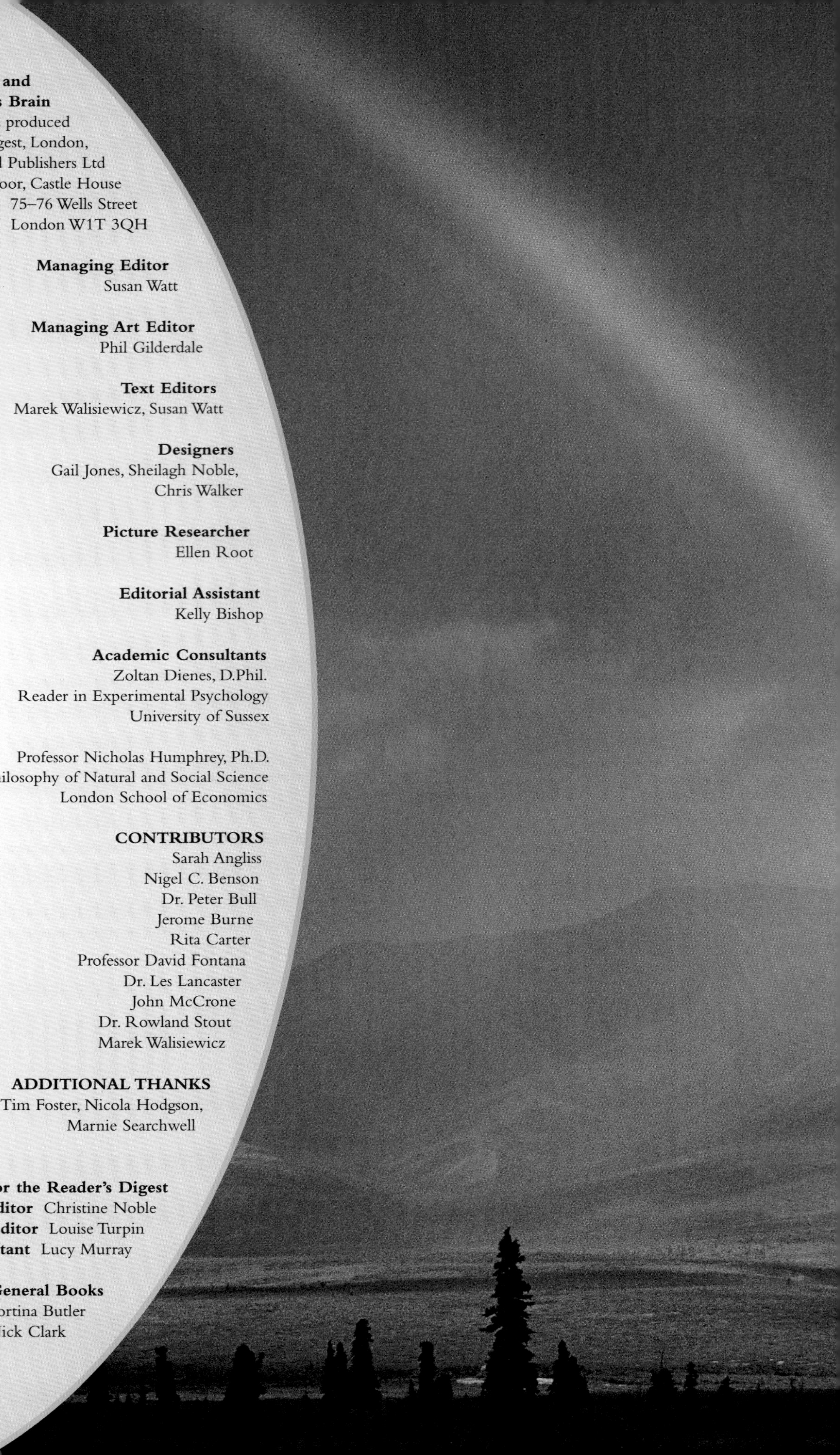

INTRODUCTION

The potential of the human brain is vast, yet most of us never stretch our own brains beyond a fraction of that potential. The *Brain Power* series contains a wealth of fascinating information, exercises and tips to enable you to understand your brain better and find out how you can use it to improve your life, whatever your age. Once you realise what your brain is capable of achieving, you'll be able to improve your memory, enhance your intelligence, increase your creativity and much more. The quest to understand consciousness is one of the burning issues of brain science today. Another is how our conscious and unconscious minds work together to produce our thoughts and actions. *The Conscious and Unconscious Brain* explores these issues and reveals recent discoveries about the workings of the brain. It explains how to tap into the power of your own unconscious, and describes techniques that can enhance your conscious awareness and help you to achieve a more focused mind. You only live life once, so make sure you're fully 'there' while you're living it.

BRAIN POWER • THE CONSCIOUS AND UNCONSCIOUS BRAIN

THE MIRACLE OF CONSCIOUSNESS

Consciousness is the most remarkable product of the human brain. It is the medium for our thoughts, and gives meaning to our experiences. Without it we could not experience sight or sound, taste, touch or smell; and from it comes our very sense of identity. Consciousness is so multi-faceted that no single definition can do it justice, but we can start by looking at some of its amazing characteristics.

WITHOUT CONSCIOUS PERCEPTION, RAINBOWS WOULD NOT HAVE ANY COLOURS

The colours we see are produced in our eyes and brains. Sunlight is split into different wavelengths when it passes through raindrops – but to see this spectrum of wavelengths as a spectrum of colours requires a conscious mind.

CERTAIN LAWS OF PHYSICS ARE BUILT INTO THE HUMAN BRAIN

Children do not have to learn that physical objects cannot disappear, or that they cannot be in two places at once. This knowledge simply appears in their minds at around the age of eight to ten months, when brain areas related to processing information about the world reach maturity.

CONSCIOUSNESS STEPS IN ONLY WHEN IT IS NEEDED

A skilled tennis player does not consciously work out where to place her racquet or feet when playing a shot. Only when a ball presents a special problem does conscious decision-making come into play.

THE HUMAN BRAIN HAS A BUILT-IN AWARENESS OF OTHER PEOPLE'S THOUGHTS

An intuitive awareness of other people's thinking and their view of situations develops in children at around the age of four. Before this age, children usually assume that others have the same information and feelings as themselves. This 'mind-reading' ability is located in the frontal lobes of the brain.

YOUR BRAIN AUTOMATICALLY 'ZOOMS IN' ON IMPORTANT INFORMATION

If your name is spoken quietly, even amid the loud babble of conversation at a party, you will hear it and be able to tune into the person saying it. The brain accomplishes this by processing incoming information at an unconscious level, and may bring significant information to consciousness.

YOUR BRAIN NEVER STOPS WORKING, EVEN WHEN YOU ARE ASLEEP

Even in deep sleep, there is activity in parts of the brain, including the cortex. Overall, there is practically no difference in total brain activity during a period of sleep and one of wakefulness.

YOU CAN RESPOND TO A STIMULUS BEFORE YOU ARE EVEN CONSCIOUS OF IT

It takes about a fifth of a second for you to become aware of a visual stimulus, such as a ball thrown towards you. But within a tenth of a second your brain has calculated what you need to do to catch it, and started off the process.

THE BRAIN CREATES OUR SENSE OF TIME BY DIVIDING THE FLOW OF EVENTS INTO A SEQUENCE OF FRAMES

A normal brain detects about ten events per second. The brain's 'clock' mechanism is based on the regular rate at which certain brain cells fire. Damage to the brain area involved can make time appear to slow down or speed up.

YOUR BRAIN REMEMBERS A FACE – EVEN IF YOU CLAIM NOT TO HAVE SEEN IT

If a photograph of a face is flashed onto a screen in front of your eyes for about one tenth of a second, it does not have time to enter your conscious awareness. However, if you encounter the same image later, your body will respond to it as though it is familiar.

A CAPACITY FOR SPIRITUAL EXPERIENCE IS WIRED INTO THE HUMAN BRAIN

Certain areas of the brain's temporal and frontal lobes produce feelings of transcendence (like experiences of religious ecstasy) when they are stimulated. This suggests we may be drawn to explore the religious and spiritual dimensions of life because of the way our brains are constructed.

1 WHAT IS CONSCIOUSNESS?

Consciousness is one of those enigmatic words: we use it happily enough in conversation, but as soon as we stop to think about what it really means, it seems impossible to pin it down. Even the experts – philosophers, psychologists, neuroscientists – seem to hit this problem and opinions vary dramatically: some think it may be the fundamental stuff of the universe, the defining characteristic of what it is to be human, while others see it as no more than a fiction, a by-product of the physical interaction of cells.

The quest to understand the nature of consciousness raises some fascinating questions. If consciousness springs from the brain, can we see it in operation in brain scans? Is it a uniquely human attribute, or do animals possess consciousness of a kind? Computers are becoming ever-more powerful, so is it just a matter of time before a machine emerges with a conscious mind?

Astonishing ingenuity has gone into investigating such questions, from many different perspectives. What is clear is that we are still at the beginning of an exciting journey of discovery not just to understand consciousness, but to understand ourselves.

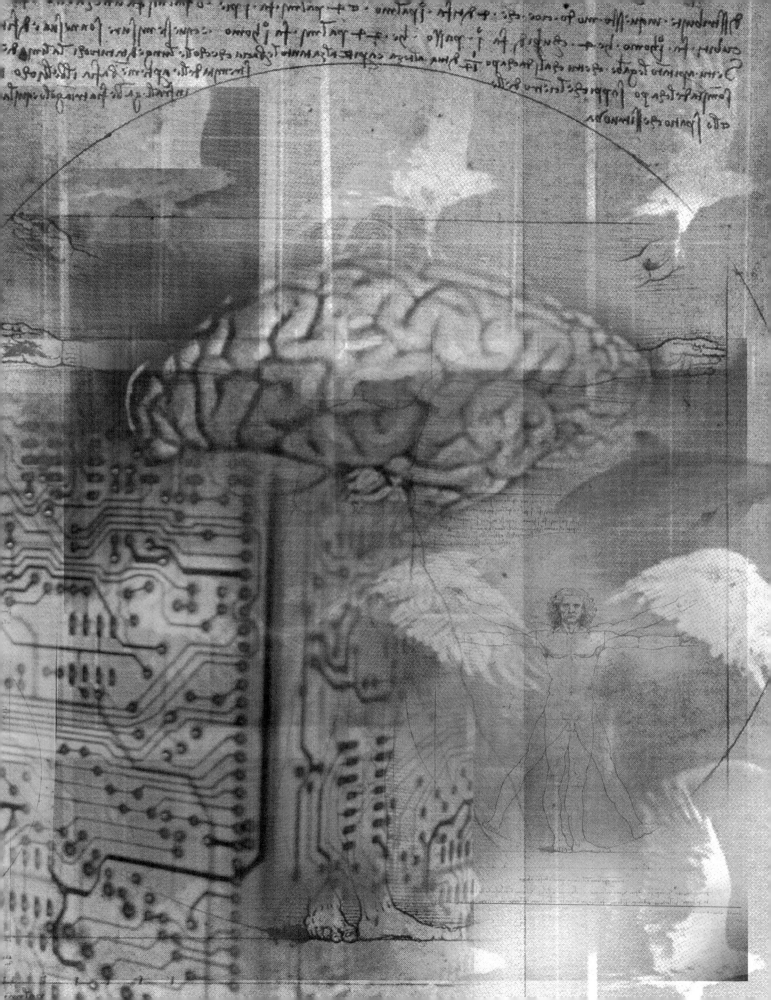

THE ENIGMA OF CONSCIOUSNESS

Although no one knows exactly what consciousness is, there are many different theories. Some of them are thousands of years old, while some are new ideas conceived by explorations at the frontiers of philosophy and neuroscience.

Consciousness is a puzzle. For a start, we all use the words 'consciousness' and 'conscious' to mean many different things. For example, we may say that we are conscious of someone or something, meaning that we are aware of that person, idea or object; but this is not the same as simply being conscious. This variety of meanings, and the difficulty of pinning down what we are referring to when we use the word 'conscious', is part of the reason why it is so hard to say exactly what consciousness is.

Even trying to separate the states in which we are conscious from those in which we are not is not straightforward. If you are in a deep, dreamless sleep, you are unconscious – and if you are wide awake and enjoying your experience of the world, you are conscious. This seems clear, but there are borderline cases.

Brain and mind
Smelling and seeing a flower may lead us to think of buying a bouquet for a friend, or remind us of a happy memory. But how do our brain states – which are governed by physical laws – link to our train of thought, which seems to have its own logic? It is not clear that even detailed brain scans could answer this question.

During the process of falling asleep you may be neither fully conscious nor unconscious. And when you are dreaming you seem to be having experiences of some sort, but are you conscious in quite the same way as when you are awake?

Among philosophers and psychologists who study consciousness, there are also many different opinions in answer to the question 'what is consciousness?' One reason why consciousness is so puzzling is that while it certainly depends on the brain, it seems to be a very different sort of thing from what is actually going on in the brain in terms of brain cell activity. For example, when a flower is present in your consciousness, there is nothing remotely like a flower actually in your brain. And the links that your mind makes from one conscious thought or image to another seem to follow a logic that does not correspond to the physical laws that govern brain processes.

Mental and physical realms

This kind of reasoning has led some philosophers to think of consciousness as a non-physical thing – a sort of spiritual container in which your thoughts, emotions, experiences and so on take place. They have argued that you have unique access to your own consciousness-container: only you can look inside it and your knowledge of its contents is infallible. There is no part of the physical world which you have this special access to. For example, a neuroscientist may have much better knowledge of what is going on inside your brain from a physical point of view than you do – but he or she would still have no access to your conscious experiences. It seems to follow, therefore, that your consciousness is not part of the physical world.

René Descartes (1596–1650) was one philosopher who thought of consciousness in this way. The philosophical theory named after him, Cartesian dualism, separates the world into two distinct realms – the physical realm inhabited by atoms, molecules, tables, chairs and human bodies, and the mental realm which souls inhabit and where conscious thoughts and experiences take place.

One major problem with this view is that the two realms cannot be regarded as entirely separate from one another since, as we all know, the body affects the mind and the mind affects the body. When we perceive things, our conscious experiences are affected by events in our sense

> **"Each one of us has only our own thoughts and feelings and no one else's. From the first-person point of view, the great divide is between what is me and what is not me."**
>
> Owen Flanagan, professor of philosophy

MODERN THEORIES OF CONSCIOUSNESS

Here are some of the most influential ways in which consciousness has been described by experts. Many other theories lie between and beyond these positions.

- **Idealism**
'Mind' or 'spirit' is the only thing that really exists – the material universe is an illusion produced by it. Consciousness therefore does not need to be explained in physical terms.

- **Functionalism**
Consciousness is not a separate thing, but a way of ordering the physical world. A brain is conscious because it is processing information in a certain way and consciousness is wholly material.

- **Identity**
The physical brain activity associated with consciousness is consciousness. There is no need to explain the link between mind and brain because there is no link – they are one and the same.

- **Eliminativism**
Consciousness does not exist as a 'thing'. We think we are conscious, but it is an illusion. Close scrutiny of what we take to be experience from the senses reveals that it is essentially no different from the knowledge we hold unconsciously.

- **Quantum approaches**
Consciousness is the manifestation of quantum effects in the brain and differs from any other observable part of the natural world because it is not bound by the same physical laws.

organs, and when we decide to act our conscious thoughts affect our muscles and limbs. If the mental realm were totally separate from the physical world and did not even exist in space, how could it interact with and have an effect on the body? And what would happen at the intersection between mind and body, between the non-physical and physical realms? Any process that could cross this intersection – and thus provide the causal link between mind and body that we all experience – would have to be a material process on one side and a non-material process on the other, which seems impossible. Most philosophers today no longer regard Cartesian dualism as a possible solution to the relationship between the mental realm of consciousness and the physical world.

Emerging powers

So what is the alternative? Most thinkers now agree that there is no need to believe that consciousness is in fact something distinct from the activity of the physical brain. Rather, consciousness can be regarded as an 'emergent property' of the brain, a characteristic that arises out of the combined action of its highly complex parts, and occurs only when these parts are functioning together. It is not a feature of the brain that can be observed with a microscope; but nor is it in a realm of its own.

As an analogy, consider a painting of a landscape. The fact that it is a

THINK AGAIN!   THE IMPOSSIBLE QUESTION

Some present-day philosophers think that it is impossible to give a valid answer to the question 'What is consciousness?'. Two prominent exponents of such views are Colin McGinn and David Chalmers.

Colin McGinn argues that there must be some natural property of the brain that is responsible for consciousness, but that we are cut off by our own cognitive limitations from ever being able to understand the relationship between the brain and consciousness. We are like five-year-old children faced with the task of understanding relativity theory. We are in this situation because the only way we have of getting access to our conscious experience is by introspection, but introspection is not a faculty that can give us any understanding of the brain. External perception and scientific investigation give us our understanding of brains. But we do not have any faculty that can put introspection and external perception together to give us an understanding of consciousness and brains together.

David Chalmers is less pessimistic. He argues that no theory of consciousness in terms of neuroscience is possible, but that it may be possible to construct a theory that explains the relationship between the brain and consciousness – if we use consciousness, not the brain, as the starting point. This theory would include the concept of experience as a basic term – just as theories in physics use the concepts of mass, charge, and so on as basic – rather than neurons or other brain science concepts. So we would need a new type of science in order to express the relationship between consciousness and brains.

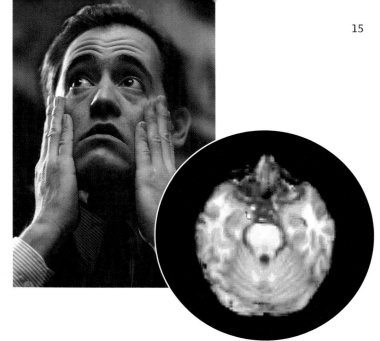

painting of a landscape cannot be observed by studying the microscopic make-up of the painting. We might be able to describe it in detail as a complex array of differently coloured pigments – but we would fail to capture the power of the painting to depict a landscape. This power is a property of the painting as a whole, not of the individual brushstrokes. It is not a separate physical thing, but emerges from the arrangement of the pigments as a distinct quality. In a similar way, although consciousness cannot be fully understood by examining the brain and its component parts, it does not exist as something over and above the brain – just as a separate quality.

Perspective and allegory

So has the riddle of consciousness now been solved? Not quite. Fundamentally, we understand consciousness through being conscious ourselves, by looking at it from the inside. But when we consider the brain, we must consider that from the outside. The difficulty of understanding consciousness in terms of brain science is in reconciling these two perspectives. Many philosophers think that, while these two perspectives describe exactly the same thing – a physical person, they do so in such different ways and using such different language that it would be impossible ever to completely express one perspective in terms of the other. So, while most thinkers throughout contemporary philosophy and psychology are agreed on a 'materialist' understanding of the mind – that is, that there is no separate mind or soul substance – they are also agreed that we will have to continue talking as if there were a separate mental realm inhabited with motives, suspicions, desires and all the other facets of our own mental experience, as these will not be found directly in the brain.

Finally, where does this leave the soul? Now that the science of the brain has made it more difficult to accept Cartesian dualism, many religious people think the idea of the soul has a mainly allegorical value. The soul may be thought of as a metaphor for what is significant in your life – what makes you special. The idea that the soul lives on after death has largely been superseded by the idea that what is unique about you will not end when you die, even though your conscious mind no longer exists. You will go on living, in a sense, in other people's lives and in what you have done while living and knowing others.

Outside and inside Strong emotions such as anxiety or fear can be read in a person's face and shown in a brain scan. But even if brain science advanced so far that we could tell from a scan exactly what someone was thinking, this would still be quite different from experiencing this from the inside.

The idea of soul This 19th-century painting by Evelyn De Morgan depicts the passing of the soul in a style that is more allegorical than literal.

MIND PUZZLES

When we start to think about our own minds, we encounter puzzles and paradoxes quite apart from the enigmas posed by consciousness itself. For example, have you ever wondered how people make the link between their own minds and the world outside? Or how people can tell what is going on in the minds of others – and whether they experience things in the same way? Throughout the centuries, such puzzles have led leading philosophers into seemingly impossible tangles. But applying some clear thinking can help to resolve these tantalising problems.

COULD YOUR LIFE BE JUST A DREAM?

Tonight you may dream that you are reading this book, and in your dream be completely convinced that this is what you are doing – even though in reality you are fast asleep in bed. This plausible possibility raises the natural question of how do you know right now that you are not in fact in a dream? Even more disturbingly, how do you know that your whole life is not a dream?

One way to answer this question is to consider how well the life you are apparently living hangs together. There may be moments when some things seem not to make much sense, but sooner or later you will find an explanation. In fact, there are explanations for almost everything in your life: if you are in London one day and in Aberdeen the next, there will be an explanation for how you got from one to the other – perhaps a train journey. Things in your life can be investigated to any level of detail, usually without inconsistency – but in a dream, you can be flying over the rooftops one moment and then be in a completely different place the next with no explanation of how you got from one to the other. Real experience is also consistent in a deeper way than in a dream – even if a completely logical dream were possible. In a dream,

all the ideas, images and events are derived from what is already in our minds, while in reality our experiences go beyond what we ourselves know about. For example, when Isaac Newton discovered the law of gravity, his new law fitted everyone's previous experience of how objects fell – although no-one had known the law before. So it makes sense to suppose that there is a real world 'out there', beyond our own mind, that is determining our experiences: our minds cannot just be making it all up.

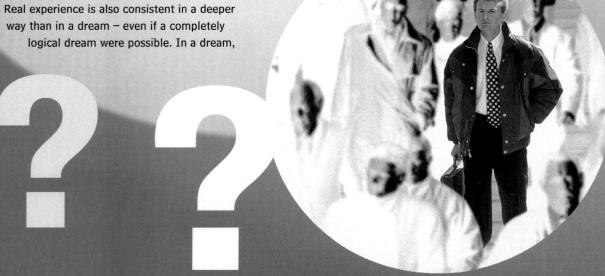

HOW DO YOU KNOW WHETHER YOUR SENSATIONS ARE THE SAME AS OTHER PEOPLE'S?

Have you ever wondered whether other people have the same experiences as you in the same situations? Perhaps you love the taste of marzipan and your friend hates it. Are you both having the same conscious experience but just reacting to it differently? Or does the marzipan taste quite differently to the two of you?

Sometimes it is clear that two people in the same situation do have quite different experiences. For example, someone who is colour blind cannot distinguish certain shades of colour that are visibly different to someone who is not colour blind. If a colour blind person hates a necktie that someone else loves, it is quite possible that this is because they are actually having different experiences of the colours in the tie.

This may apply to the taste of marzipan too. Different people's taste buds have slightly different levels of sensitivity to the various aspects of taste, so marzipan may indeed taste a little different to your friend. But it is also possible that it tastes almost exactly the same to the two of you, but you have different attitudes to it

– perhaps through associating it with different experiences in the past. Even though the marzipan tastes the same, however, it is still the case that you have different experiences of the marzipan, because your interpretation of the taste as 'nice' or 'not nice' is part of the overall experience. Your attitudes to an experience cannot really be detached from the experience itself.

So, if someone genuinely seems to have a different reaction to your own, it's likely that at a conscious level this difference is real. But this difference may lie not in your raw sensations, but in how these are interpreted and turned into conscious experiences.

CAN YOU THINK WITHOUT WORDS?

When we think, we certainly seem to use words most of the time. But are words essential for thinking, or could our minds work just as well without language?

A chess player can think through different moves and decide which one to make without putting into words all the reasoning that led to that decision. Visualisation and non-verbal thinking certainly play a part in many activities, from composing a song to cutting a key. But how different would your thinking be if you had no language at all?

Many experts think that language provides the very structure of our thinking. For example, you do not need language to see colours, but whether you perceive a colour as

'red' or 'green' surely depends on having learned these concepts through learning the words. So when you form a mental image of a red bowl, for example, you may do this without words – but your knowledge of language still plays a crucial role in pinning down exactly what you are visualising.

Grammar, too, has a powerful role in thought. It allows us to create statements and questions, and thus to say something specific about objects and events, rather than simply picking them out. A hungry cat waiting to be fed may have a vivid mental image of a plate of food, but this is not the same as having the clear belief expressed by the words 'it's time for dinner!'. Only when we have formed an explicit statement, rather than just an image, can we say – or think – whether it is true or false.

THE CONSCIOUS BRAIN

It is generally agreed today that the workings of the conscious mind – thoughts, perceptions, and awareness of emotions – are linked to physical events in the brain. But neuroscientists are only just beginning to discover how the activity of brain cells translates into the rich and multi-faceted experience of consciousness.

"The highest activities of consciousness have their origins in physical occurrences of the brain – just as the loveliest melodies are not too sublime to be expressed by notes".

W Somerset Maugham

>> CUTTING EDGE >>

POINTS OF CONSCIOUSNESS

Some brain cells are responsible for producing awareness of very specific things. Researchers used sensitive electrodes to record the activity of single neurons in the brains of monkeys. They identified one group of cells that became active only when a hand was passed from the right to the left of the animal's visual field. The cells did not respond to the hand alone, nor to any other object moving on the same course. So while consciousness emerges from the activity of the entire brain, some of its contents are due to very localised activity – right down to the level of single cells.

Whenever you are conscious, your brain cells – the neurons – are active, signalling their neighbours with regular electrochemical pulses. But this activity is not enough to explain consciousness in terms of brain activity. Even simple studies of brain activity show that neurons also fire when you are in deep sleep. Conversely, even when you are intensely conscious, most of the neural activity in your brain is linked to unconscious processing.

Imagine, for example, that you are sitting in a room reading a good book. The story is compelling and your conscious mind is filled with the action in the 'virtual' world created by your imagination. You are only dimly aware of your real surroundings – the room you are in, the hum of traffic outside, the feel of the book in your hand. And most remarkably, you are not even conscious of the process of reading. Yet all the time, your brain is processing information about these things. Millions of firing neurons tell your hand how much pressure to exert to hold the book steady. Other nerve cells perceive the shapes of the letters, discern their patterns and extract their symbolic meanings; and others still notice if anything in your environment changes, for example, if someone enters the room.

If your brain works this hard even when you are not conscious, what is so special about the neural activity of the conscious state? To answer this question, we first need to look at how the brain is organised.

Creating conscious perceptions

The human brain is a massive network of interconnected neurons. Each part of the network processes a particular type of information: some sections deal with particular emotions, others with sensory stimuli, memory, language, and so on. And within each of these sub-networks, individual neurons are specialised to deal with even more narrowly focused tasks: for example, in the visual system particular cells respond only to the colour red. The full complexity of human thought and emotion – what we call mind – arises when many of these sub-networks interact.

One theory (put forward by the DNA pioneer Francis Crick) about what happens when information is fed into this network is as follows. Imagine there is an object – say a grapefruit – in the left side of a person's visual field. The neurons concerned with this information begin to fire. These include cells that respond to the colour yellow and cells that respond to a round shape. The person – let's call her Susan – is watching television and not paying attention to the grapefruit. The 'yellow' and 'round' neurons in her brain fire relatively slowly, their activity dies away quickly, and the grapefruit does not contribute to her conscious state. But then the grapefruit captures Susan's attention. The neurons concerned get very excited, firing faster and faster. When they fire at around 40 times a second (40Hz), the 'yellow' neurons detect that the 'round' neurons are, like them, very agitated, and the two groups of neurons pool their information. The result is a perception of a 'grapefruit', rather than just of 'yellow' and 'round'. As long as the grapefruit remains the object of Susan's attention, messages will continue to flow back and forth between the two groups of neurons. If this synchrony lasts for about a fifth of a second, the grapefruit will become a conscious perception. But if the synchrony degenerates in less time, the perception will not reach Susan's consciousness, even though her brain has absorbed the information unconsciously. This sort of perception is known as 'subliminal'.

Attention and consciousness

So to be fully conscious of something – to be able to look back and know that it happened – we need to pay attention to it. Attention is rather like a searchlight: it focuses the brain on a small patch of a vast information field by enhancing activity in the neurons concerned with that patch. When we attend to something, other perceptions drop out of consciousness. The spotlight of attention is never still, so these patches of highlighted activity keep changing: at one moment the grapefruit is privileged, but soon something else takes its place. Other things may be relegated to the half-light of subliminal experience, or go entirely unnoted.

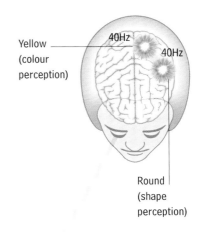

Yellow (colour perception)

40Hz

40Hz

Round (shape perception)

Seeing a grapefruit
When you notice an object like a grapefruit, specialised areas of neurons in your brain are stimulated in response to the colour yellow, while others fire in response to the round shape. Together they create your perception of the grapefruit.

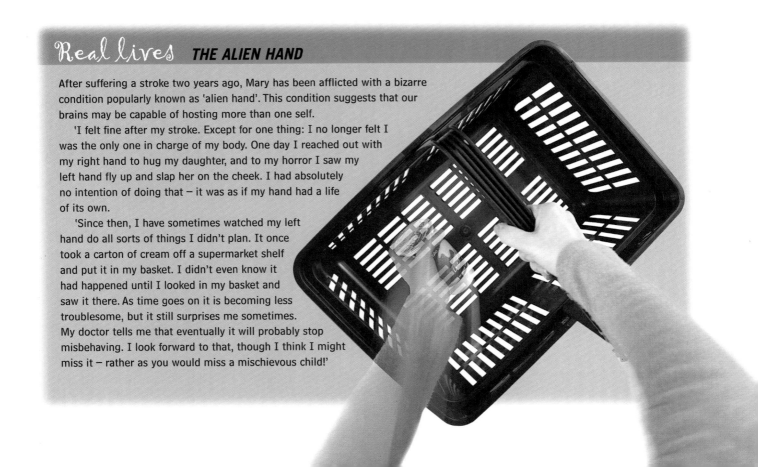

Real lives THE ALIEN HAND

After suffering a stroke two years ago, Mary has been afflicted with a bizarre condition popularly known as 'alien hand'. This condition suggests that our brains may be capable of hosting more than one self.

'I felt fine after my stroke. Except for one thing: I no longer felt I was the only one in charge of my body. One day I reached out with my right hand to hug my daughter, and to my horror I saw my left hand fly up and slap her on the cheek. I had absolutely no intention of doing that – it was as if my hand had a life of its own.

'Since then, I have sometimes watched my left hand do all sorts of things I didn't plan. It once took a carton of cream off a supermarket shelf and put it in my basket. I didn't even know it had happened until I looked in my basket and saw it there. As time goes on it is becoming less troublesome, but it still surprises me sometimes. My doctor tells me that eventually it will probably stop misbehaving. I look forward to that, though I think I might miss it – rather as you would miss a mischievous child!'

CONSCIOUSNESS AND THE BRAIN

THE CORTEX

This is the upper layer of the brain, covering each of the hemispheres. At the front are the frontal lobes, containing the prefrontal lobes and the motor cortex, which controls **body movements**. Behind this is the sensory cortex, where information from the body and senses is processed.

Frontal lobes
These are necessary for higher conscious functions, including **language-based thought**. Here, incoming information is combined with existing knowledge and becomes fully conscious. The left motor cortex contains Broca's area, where **speech production** is located. During sleep, activity in the frontal lobes is reduced.

Sensory cortex
This large area includes the primary visual, auditory and somatosensory cortex, which process raw data from the eyes, ears and body; and the sensory association areas, where this data is brought together.

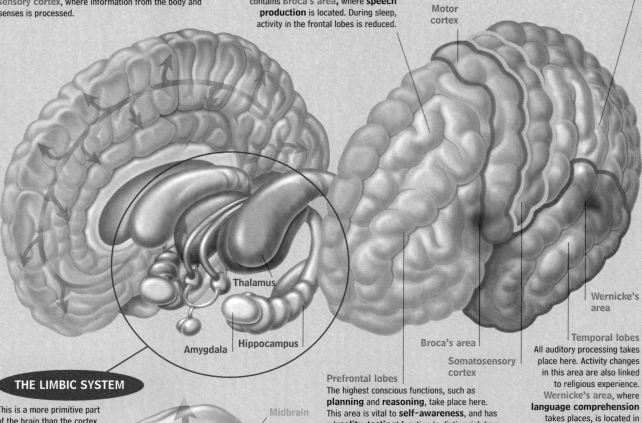

Motor cortex

Thalamus

Amygdala   Hippocampus

Wernicke's area

Broca's area

Somatosensory cortex

Temporal lobes
All auditory processing takes place here. Activity changes in this area are also linked to religious experience. Wernicke's area, where **language comprehension** takes places, is located in the left temporal lobe.

THE LIMBIC SYSTEM

This is a more primitive part of the brain than the cortex. It contains the amygdala (where **emotions** such as fear and anger are generated); the **hippocampus** (vital for encoding and retrieving **memories**, and for self-awareness); and the **thalamus,** which directs and modulates activity within the cortex.

Prefrontal lobes
The highest conscious functions, such as **planning** and **reasoning**, take place here. This area is vital to **self-awareness**, and has a '**reality-testing**' function to distinguish true perceptions from hallucinations.

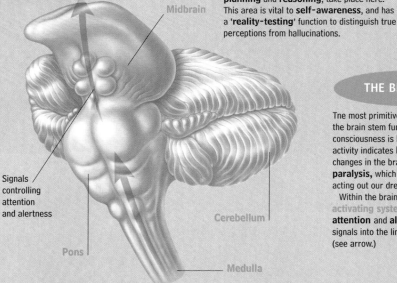

Midbrain

Signals controlling attention and alertness

Pons

Cerebellum

Medulla

THE BRAIN STEM

Tne most primitive area of the brain, the brain stem functions even when consciousness is lost; lack of brain stem activity indicates **brain death**. Activity changes in the brain stem cause **sleep paralysis,** which prevents us from acting out our dreams.

Within the brain stem, the reticular activating system (RAS), controls **attention** and **alertness** by sending signals into the limbic system and cortex (see arrow.)

The central self

The spotlight of attention flits around, yet our perceptions are bound together into our personal experience of the moment. This sense of a 'me' at the centre of perception is a crucial component of conscious experience. The brain mechanisms responsible for this sense of self are not fully understood, but they seem to reside in a circuit that runs between the frontal lobes of the brain, which deal with abstract ideas, and the language areas of the left hemisphere. This circuit weaves a continual story – the narrative self. As long as the narrative is running, experience can be integrated into the stream of consciousness (see page 102). But when these circuits are inactive, information processing in other areas of the brain ceases to be 'owned' by the individual and therefore cannot be described.

The self system creates such a strong feeling of unity that it is generally assumed that one brain can hold just one consciousness. However, some theorists believe that micro-consciousnesses may exist in every brain, rather like separate individuals. Micro-consciousnesses are, by their nature, impossible to access. If we could examine their contents, they would be brought into the stream of 'owned' consciousness and so would no longer be separate. Only under certain extraordinary circumstances, such as split-brain experiments and the 'alien hand' condition, do they come to light.

> **FACT:** Consciousness occurs when certain brain cells fire in synchrony – but if all brain cells synchronise, consciousness is lost.

(F)OCUS ON   *SPLIT BRAINS*

The human brain has two cerebral hemispheres. The left hemisphere controls the right side of the body and contains the areas involved with language, while the right hemisphere controls the left side. However, research with 'split-brain' patients – where the connections between the hemispheres have been severed for medical reasons (usually the treatment of epilepsy) – has revealed more subtle differences between the hemispheres and led some psychologists to suggest that each hemisphere contains its own separate consciousness.

In this research, the patient faces a screen with a picture on the left or right. The patient fixes their eyes on the centre of the screen, and (because of the normal crossover in the visual pathways) the visual information enters the hemisphere opposite to the side on which the picture is presented. The normal connection between the hemispheres is severed, so the information stays 'stuck' in the receiving hemisphere.

The language centres are in the left hemisphere, so the patient can describe a picture only if the information enters the left hemisphere. If it enters the right hemisphere, the patient will claim to be unaware of the image. However, if asked to select an object matching the image by touching it with the left hand (which is controlled by the right hemisphere), the patient will often succeed. When asked why they selected that object, they cannot explain. What this shows is that, while the right side of the brain appears to be unconscious because it lacks verbal ability, in fact it is capable of sophisticated cognition.

One study bears out this conclusion. Researchers devised a way of 'talking' exclusively to the right brain of a split-brain patient known as PS, by giving his left hand Scrabble letters to spell out messages from the right side of his brain. PS was asked what plans he had for his career. His spoken answer – that he intended to be a draughtsman – was provided by his left hemisphere (where the brain's language capacity is primarily located). In response to the same question, his right hemisphere gave a different answer, spelling out the words: 'automobile drive[r]'. This newly revealed ambition could be the desire of a separate consciousness in the right hemisphere – which, in normal circumstances, was unknown even to the boy himself.

ANIMAL CONSCIOUSNESS

Is a chimpanzee conscious? Or your cat or dog? What about a goldfish, prawn, or wasp? Most of us will only begin to waver with goldfish. But scientists and philosophers have often seemed strangely keen to deny a mental life to any animal.

FACT: Chimpanzees, orang-utans and dolphins are the only animals known to be able to recognise their own reflection in a mirror. Other 'intelligent' animals, such as gorillas, dogs and elephants, fail the test.

René Descartes usually gets the blame for the way we think about animal consciousness. The 17th-century French philosopher lived briefly in St Germain, a suburb of Paris. There he saw the town's famed waterwork statues of characters from Greek myth. Intricate hydraulic machinery would cause a figure of the bathing Diana to hide herself as a visitor approached. A few steps closer, and more hydraulic trickery would reveal a fierce, trident-waving Neptune.

These clever statues inspired Descartes to argue that living animals were also just contrivances. Earlier philosophers, taking their lead from Aristotle, had been quite happy to grant animals a sensitive soul, if not a rational one – consciousness if not cognition. But Descartes said the brain and the body's nervous system were just a hydraulic network and that animal behaviour was purely based on reflexes – there was no mind involved. According to Descartes, only humans possessed the extra component in the midst of all this machinery that could endow the ability to think, speak and reflect. That component was the soul.

Descartes' idea stuck, partly because it fitted in with Church doctrine. And even scientists felt it was justifiable to regard animals as bundles of reflexes, rather than credit them with a consciousness that could not actually be seen or measured.

Inside the animal mind

Descartes' view of animal consciousness has now been largely rejected because it seems obvious that animals think and feel. Anyone can see the light of intelligent awareness in the eyes of a

dolphin, dog or chimpanzee. However, experts still agree that the animal mind is limited. One answer suggested by philosophers as various as Schopenhauer and Locke is that animals are conscious, but their consciousness is locked into the present tense. Or as some psychologists have more recently put it, animals cannot think 'off-line'. All their responses are associative, being connected to the immediate demands and potentials of the moment.

Watch a cat lazing on a sunny lawn. It is conscious of the bees buzzing, the smells wafting on the breeze, the contented feel of a full belly. But you probably do not think it is reflecting on its kittenhood, or planning revenge on the old tom next door, or wondering whether it is having fish or chicken for supper. The cat is vividly aware of life and ready to respond if something disturbs it. But it does not seem to have an inner mechanism for directing its mind away from the moment to ponder the past or ruminate about the future.

However, these off-line capabilities apart, psychologists have found that the thought and memory capacities of animals are remarkably similar to humans. For instance, much has been made of the fact that animals lack insight and have to have lessons drummed in reflexively. But even goldfish and toads prove capable of one-shot learning. Toads only make the mistake of snapping at a bumblebee once, and a single electric shock is enough to make a goldfish reluctant to swim towards a corner of a tank. Chimpanzees were once thought to be exceptional because they were capable of making creative leaps of thought – for example, realising that a crate could be dragged across a floor to serve as a platform to stand on

THINK AGAIN!

CHICKENS HAVE FEELINGS TOO

In one study, scientists tested what chickens really want by making them squeeze through tight gaps in a fence in order to get different things. High on the chicken wish list proved to be a quiet nest box for egg laying and access to dirt or woodshavings for scratching about in. Surprisingly, chickens were not desperate to rejoin their flock. And when kind-hearted researchers tried to prove that factory-farmed hens ought to have a thicker, more comfortable, gauge of wire netting for the flooring of their cages, the birds contradicted them, showing a preference for the old thinner wire.

▶▶ CUTTING EDGE ▶▶ ANTS – A COLLECTIVE MIND?

Individually, an ant is a rather limited creature. But collectively, do ants form a group mind? After all, an ant nest is almost one organism genetically, a single queen living with as many as a million daughters. And all those eyes and jaws are linked like brain cells in a network of interactions that can respond to the world with sharp intelligence.

Watch a trail of ants and you will see they are forever bumping into each other, pausing to touch antennae. In every brief meeting they exchange information about what they are doing. Their tiny brains then apply some simple rules. If an ant finds it is rarely meeting another employed in the same task (or too many others doing the same task) it will switch to a different behaviour. So from nest maintenance to foraging, ants spread themselves out across their territory, doing what needs to be done as if the colony were conscious as a whole.

Deborah Gordon of Stanford University studies

Harvester ants in the Arizona desert, and has found that colonies develop more intelligence as they mature. A colony sticks to the same sized territory as it grows in number, thereby creating a web of interactions that becomes ever denser and smarter. When Gordon set problems by blocking foraging trails or messing up the nest site with toothpicks, she found that mature colonies were quicker and more reliable in their response. Younger colonies were erratic in their behaviour as if they had not quite learnt what to do. The older colonies had also discovered how to get along with their neighbours. If foraging trails happened to cross one day, next day the ants would head in the opposite direction. But adolescent colonies always returned looking for a fight.

The evidence suggests that there is a sort of collective intelligence at work in an ant trail. Like a human mind, the trail 'knows' the world.

UNDERSTANDING YOUR PET: FACTS AND FALLACIES

Q: Why is my cat so surprised when a ball drops in front of it?
A: The cat's eye is very sensitive to horizontal motion – try rolling a ball across the floor – but surprisingly blind to vertical motion.

Q: When a bloodhound finds a trail, how does it know which way to head?
A: Its nose is sensitive enough to tell which of two footsteps is a split second fresher.

Q: Why does my cat insist on sitting on the kitchen counter?
A: Some breeds like the Singapura and the Siamese are natural climbers that like to view life from a perch.

Q: Is my dog colour blind?
A: No, just limited in colour sensitivity. Dogs can tell reds from blues, but reds and greens, or blues and purples, look much the same.

Q: Why does my parrot regurgitate on me?
A: In parrots, this is a sign of love! Bonded birds show their affection by feeding each other like they feed their chicks.

Q: What is the smartest – and the dumbest – breed of dog?
A: Collies, poodles and German shepherds are among the brightest – some can learn a new command after just five repetitions. In contrast, some afghans, bulldogs and basenjis may take hundreds.

Q: Why does my cat head straight for a friend who hates cats?
A: Direct eye contact and shrill baby-talk can be threatening to a cat, so they often prefer those who offer a cold shoulder.

Q: What kind of TV do pets like?
A: Golf, or anything with moving balls, is popular with kittens. Dogs like to watch other dogs. And parrots seem to like anything noisy with lots of gunfire.

HOW TO READ A CAT'S TAIL

Cats make more than one hundred different vocal sounds – ten times more than dogs. They also convey a lot of meaning through their swishing tails. Here is how to read some of the signs.

1 Tail raised slightly: cat is interested in something.
2 Tail erect, tip tilted: cat is friendly with slight reservations.
3 Tail fully erect, tip stiff: intense friendly greeting with no reservations.
4 Tail held still, tip twitching: mild irritation.
5 Tail swishing violently: cat about to attack.
6 Tail raised and fluffed out: cat is aggressive.

HOW TO BE TOP DOG IN YOUR OWN HOME

Dogs and humans have a long history – more than 100,000 years compared with less than 10,000 years for other domesticated animals. But as former pack animals, dogs need to know where they rank in your family.

Handing over scraps of your own dinner to a demanding mutt can be a very bad idea, leading it to think that it is actually 'top dog'. So is giving in when your dog decides to sit in your armchair. But a dog that is relegated to the bottom of the bed or a place at your feet will learn to be happy in this subordinate position. At the edge of the human 'camp' is his most natural place.

The natural way to stop a dog barking is to mimic the way a mother wolf silences a noisy cub by grasping its muzzle gently in her jaws and growling a low warning. Wrap a hand over your dog's muzzle and firmly say 'Quiet,' until it gets the message.

7 Tail lowered and fluffed out: cat is afraid.
8 Tail held to one side: sexual invitation of a female cat in heat.

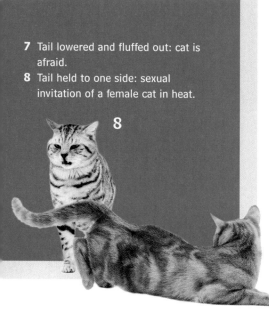

Eagle eye The sensory world of animals is very different to our own. An eagle's eyes are eight times more densely packed with light-detecting cells. It also sees extra colours because its eye samples light at four wavebands rather than just our three.

to reach a dangling banana. But then pigeons were found also to be capable of apparently sudden insight on similar set-ups, if they were given appropriate training.

Of course, brain size makes a difference: goldfish can remember which way to swim to reach a reward of food for only about ten seconds; pigeons and lizards can remember such information for minutes; apes for hours. Nevertheless, it seems that the general set of mental skills is much the same across the animal kingdom. Even slugs and insects have some degree of memory or learning ability.

What's it like to be a dolphin?

While the mental abilities of animals are often remarkable, in many respects, animal consciousness is very different from our own. Unlike humans, with their faculties of self-criticism and reflection, animals are thought to live their subjective lives forever in the present, and the present that they inhabit may be very different from human experience. For example, what would it be like to be a dolphin perceiving the world through sonar? Like bats, dolphins emit ultra sonic clicks and build up a picture of their surroundings from the echoes. With their clicks pitched at frequencies of up to 100,000 hertz, dolphins can 'see' right through soft structures as if they had ultrasound scanners. Passing a pregnant swimmer, a dolphin would also see the baby wriggling inside. Or what about being able to feel the pressure of the Earth's magnetic field like a migrating bird? Many birds (as well as mice, dolphins, bees, frogs and even bacteria) seem able to navigate using an inbuilt compass.

The phenomenal worlds of animals – what it is actually like to sense and perceive as another species – may vary remarkably, but confined to our own consciousness we cannot know what it is like to be a dolphin or what it feels like to be a bird.

Evolution of human consciousness

How did the animal mind turn into the self-aware human mind? What change occurred, freeing us to think objectively and introspectively? Language, it seems, may have been the key.

Experts agree that the development of human consciousness in all its modern complexity happened astonishingly quickly. For millions of years, early human species had existed as large-brained, bipedal apes. Our direct forebears, *Homo erectus,* could make fires and tools, but these were crude and simple. Then, 150,000 years ago, our own species, *Homo sapiens,* emerged. Just 100,000 years later – a blink of the eye in evolutionary terms – *Homo sapiens* had transfomed itself into the linguistic, highly cultured, fully conscious species we are today.

In this brief time, our tools became finely crafted and technically advanced. We could carve fish hooks and harpoon tips, make ropes and sew clothes, and we mastered fire using hearths, flint lighters and fat-burning lamps. Most significantly, we began using symbols to represent our world. We adorned our bodies, carved statuettes and painted the walls of our caves. Archaeological evidence reveals that our lives became ruled by memories, hopes, beliefs and fears. We had indisputably become modern in our mental abilities.

Willendorf Venus
This statuette symbolising fertility was made about 30,000 years ago.

Better, not bigger

What could explain such a swift transformation? It certainly was not just an increase in brain size: the Neanderthals (*Homo neanderthalensis*), who lived alongside *Homo sapiens* until about 30,000 years ago, had slightly bigger brains but showed little sign of intellectual sophistication. So what did change?

Theorists are divided: some think that an overall change in the organisation of the brain was responsible, while others believe that a single factor – language – holds the key. The overall change theorists suggest that the brains of our apeman ancestors gradually accumulated a range of separate mental skills, such as tool-making, foraging and social behaviour. Then, later, these skills became linked, so whereas before we could employ our tool-using 'module' only to visualise the handling of tools, afterwards, we could use it to manipulate information stored anywhere in the brain.

One drawback of this theory is that there is little evidence that brains are, or ever were, so rigidly

***Homo sapiens* skull** This skull from Ethiopia dates from 100,000 years ago.

150,000 years ago
First *Homo sapiens* appeared

Timeline of culture and consciousness Bipedal ape species date back to 4 or 5 million years ago, but our own species, *Homo sapiens*, first appeared relatively recently (about 150,000 years ago). 100,000 years later, a cultural explosion began: works of art appeared, technology advanced rapidly and complex societies emerged. Language – and through it, consciousness – may have been the key to these crucial steps in the evolution of modern humans.

Ancient cave art This artistically accomplished painting of a horse was discovered in the caves at Lascaux in France, and dates from about 35,000 years ago.

divided into modules. This lends weight to the idea that the power of our brains was unlocked by a single factor – the evolution of language. Anatomical evidence is consistent with this idea. While Neanderthals retained an ape-like vocal tract, early *Homo sapiens* had the arched palate, voice box, and other adaptations needed to speak articulately. But how could our use of language spark the explosive spiral of cultural and technological development that is so evident in the archaeological record of our species?

Talking the talk

The explanation goes like this: while animals have general intelligence, they can direct this intelligence only towards the events of the moment. Words, on the other hand, can bring buried knowledge to mind. Hearing (or saying to yourself) a phrase like 'fat rhinoceros in a pink tutu' will instantly conjure up an image that would otherwise not have been present in your head. And when the symbolic reach of words is combined with the logical engine of grammar, then our thoughts can really begin to go somewhere. So according to some language theorists, there was no great change in our consciousness or intelligence.

Instead, just a minor evolutionary step in the brains of our ancestors – the ability to process grammar – allowed humans to use speech to corral mental images and rouse memories. The result was a step change in our ability to direct our thoughts to wherever we wanted them to go. We became the explorers of our own minds.

But the question that still needs to be answered is what evolutionary advantage did we gain through our ability to examine our own thoughts? Again, answers are speculative, but perhaps one of the most convincing explanations for the evolution of the 'inner eye' was that it allowed us to know what others were thinking. By examining our own thoughts and feelings, we could make informed guesses about the motivations – and therefore the possible actions – of other members of our social group. So consciousness made us all into psychologists, and opened up a whole new arena of human behaviour – sympathy, compassion, jealousy, trust, deviousness, belief and disbelief.

Bone whistle This was carved from a reindeer's toe bone 40,000 years ago.

Flint tool This beautifully worked blade is 20,000 years old.

Pictographic writing This Sumerian clay tablet dates from 3000 BC.

60,000 years ago First orderly campsites

40,000 years ago First lamps, statuettes and shaped bone tools

35,000 years ago First cave paintings and spear heads

20,000 years ago First bows and arrows, cloth and sewing needles

15,000 years ago First domestic animals

10,000 years ago First villages and crop planting

5000 years ago First cities and writing

CONSCIOUSNESS AND MACHINES

Could a machine ever be conscious? Many experts say 'yes, of course', believing that technology will one day be able to produce a machine with a mind of its own. But these experts have been proved wrong in the past – and according to earlier predictions, conscious machines should exist by now.

FACT: If computer power keeps doubling every two years, then the desktop machines of 2050 will be about 15 million times more powerful than today's – surely enough for machine intelligence, if not consciousness?

If you simulated a weather pattern on a computer, would it be real weather? Would its wind ruffle your hair or its rain make you wet? No, of course not, no matter how exact and complete the simulation. So then why would you expect a simulation of your brain processes to be really conscious? On the other hand, think about this. Suppose just one of your brain cells was replaced with a microchip that did exactly the same job. If all the inputs and outputs remained precisely the same, you would never notice the difference. And what if another, then another, cell was replaced, until gradually all 100 billion neurons in your brain had been turned to silicon. Would there ever come a point where you stopped being you? Would you become, in effect, a conscious machine?

These are exactly the kind of questions that cognitive scientists have been throwing at each other since the dawn of the computer era. Even now, science does not seem much closer to answering them.

Applying some logic

Alan Turing, the British mathematician who laid the foundations of modern computing in the 1940s, firmly believed that machines would be able to think for themselves sooner rather than later, and certainly by the

PIONEERS ALAN TURING

Alan Turing's life was brilliant and tragic in equal measure. Born in 1912, the son of a civil servant in India, his childhood was a lonely mix of boarding schools and holiday foster homes back in England. In 1937, as a young don at Cambridge University, he published a short paper that at a stroke established the universal mathematical principles behind computers. Then, with the outbreak of World War II, he was recruited to help develop the first code-cracking machines at Bletchley Park, a top-secret intelligence centre in the UK.

After the war, Turing hoped to perfect his designs for a true general-purpose computer. However, this project fell foul of bureaucracy and technical delays, so Turing returned to theoretical visions of future

machines. In 1950, he made his famous forecast that computers would soon think, tickling the public with blithe comments like: 'One day ladies will take their computers for walks in the park and tell each other, "My little computer said such a funny thing this morning!"'

Unfortunately for Turing, when police officers were investigating a robbery at his house in 1952, he accidentally revealed that he was homosexual – which was then illegal. Turing was convicted of gross indecency and only spared a prison sentence on the condition that he took a 'curative' course of female hormone injections. In 1954, aged 41, he committed suicide by eating an apple laced with cyanide.

end of the 20th century. Turing's breakthrough was to prove that, in theory, the simplest computing device – he imagined a single key making or erasing marks in succession on an infinite tape – could carry out any logically defined operation. All computers were therefore identical under the skin, as their workings could always be described in terms of this theoretical device (which became known as a Turing machine). You could build a computer out of anything, even string and old tin cans. While it might not be very efficient or fast, the output of its programs would remain the same. Turing offered mathematical proof that if you could describe the 'programs' being run on the human brain, then the same programs could be run on an artificial brain. He did not think that the technology of his day would have to be scaled up much to run the basic programs of human consciousness at useful speeds.

There was, as Turing himself admitted, a potential problem with this argument, which lay in whether the brain's operations were indeed logical. Could whatever brains did actually be represented as a binary sequence of 0s and 1s? But like most scientists, Turing was optimistic, because brain cells seemed to communicate using on-off patterns of electrical spikes.

So there was a clever intellectual trick at the heart of Turing's argument. He had proved that, in mathematical terms, all computers were essentially the same. Now it was up to others to prove that human brains were not computers. This was, and remains, a very difficult task. Anyone who draws a categorical distinction between the logical workings of a brain and those of a computer can always be undermined – they simply have not considered every last alternative or explored every fact. While you can show that machine consciousness is highly unlikely or impractical, scientifically speaking you cannot remove the doubt about whether it might be done in the future based on some as yet undiscovered fact.

FOCUS ON THE TURING TEST

Working on the principle of that if something walks like a duck and quacks like a duck then it is a duck, Alan Turing once suggested that the only test of consciousness that a computer would have to pass is to convince a human that it is also conscious.

This rather tongue-in-cheek idea has sparked an annual contest in which judges, conversing via a keyboard and screen, have to guess whether they are chatting to an artificial intelligence program or real person. No program has yet duped the judges even though their questions are hardly probing. Would you be fooled by this conversation?

Computer: Hello. My name is Jim. Who are you?
Judge: Charles.
Computer: Charles is a wrestler in As You Like It. Charles is King of France in Henry VI Pt 1.
Judge: Do you like Shakespeare?
Computer: Yeah, sure.
Judge: What do you like about his plays?
Computer: Well, there's a certain je ne sais quoi.
Judge: I think it is great that you like his plays.
Computer: I like phasers.
Judge: Do you mean like those in Star Trek?
Computer: It's possible.
Judge: What's possible?
Computer: Nothing.
Judge: That's a very nihilistic stance.
Computer: Indeed.

"The point is not that the computer gets only to the 40-yard line and not all the way to the goal line. The computer doesn't even get started. It is not playing the game."

John Searle, professor of philosophy

Chinese whispers

Philosophers, of course, have made valiant attempts to come up with just such an 'in principle' argument against machine consciousness. The most famous of these is the Chinese Room thought experiment of US philosopher John Searle.

Searle asks us to imagine a man locked in a room. He does not understand Chinese, but he is surrounded by millions of books that give the precise answer to every possible question framed in that language. From time to time, someone shoves a query written in Chinese through a slot. The man's job is to rifle through the books, find a match to the question, then scribble back the prescribed reply. From the outside, the room appears to have an intelligent comprehension of Chinese. And yet we know that inside there is just a man following rules without having the slightest clue about the meaning of either the question or the response. Searle says that exactly the same would be the case with a computer. It might run a program and output realistic behaviour. But there would be no inner light of experience or understanding. A computer has rules, but not semantics – that is, inner knowledge of what in the real world is being manipulated by those rules.

But the computer scientists disagree with this viewpoint. They say that our brains have semantics and true understanding because they manipulate mental representations – broad washes of sensation and memory displayed across millions of brain cells. So the correct way to imagine the Chinese Room is as many little men, each representing points of data in a co-ordinated show. Like individual brain cells, each tiny figure would merely follow local processing rules. But the network as a whole would be conscious. As a system, the Chinese Room really would 'feel' that it understood the questions.

▶▶ CUTTING EDGE ▶▶ A CONSCIOUS INTERNET?

What if the internet one day grew so connected that it woke up and became conscious? Some experts think this could really happen. Belgian computer scientist Francis Heylighen argues that web pages are like information-containing brain cells, and the hyperlinks between them are like synaptic connections between brain cells. Throw in search engines and other kinds of intelligent programs and perhaps the whole thing could start to come alive.

It's an interesting idea. However, the more sober-minded point out that machines are best seen as amplifiers of human activity. The Industrial Revolution was about the amplification of human muscle power. Today's information revolution is about the amplification of human mental power. So while the internet does promise remarkable things, the real story will not be its emerging consciousness, but how it will extend the reach of our own minds into a global, shareable body of knowledge and culture.

Again, the argument is one that the anti-computer camp seemingly cannot win. Searle has continued to blaze away, objecting that simulated weather will never make you wet and a simulated carburettor will never power a car. Simulations cannot have real effects on the world. But computer scientists reply that a weather model hooked up to your garden sprinkler would certainly make you wet. And in the same way, an artificial brain equipped with eyes to see and hands to act could be just as much a part of the world as you.

On the basis of this line of argument at least, there seems no good reason to rule out the possibility of machine consciousness in principle. On the other hand, 50 years of intensive but largely fruitless research has shown that Turing and many others were wildly optimistic in their forecasts for machine intelligence, let alone machine consciousness.

The unrealised dream

During the 1970s and 1980s, huge amounts of money were ploughed into artificial intelligence (AI) research by governments, industry and especially defence research agencies. Japan, Europe and the US became locked into an intellectual arms race. The reasoning was that if the technocrats failed to deliver the conscious machines they were promising, then even slightly smart ones would have valuable applications. History tells us that the AI movement was largely unproductive. It did give us one or two clever new programming tricks, but the commercial computers of today are much the same as those of yesteryear – the main difference is that they are smaller, cheaper and faster.

There are still die-hards who insist that a major breakthrough is waiting round the corner. They point to the promise of neural networks – computers designed in direct imitation of brain networks. These may have the equivalent of only a few thousand brain cells at present (about enough to power a cockroach), but it might be just 30 or 40 years before such a computer has enough connections to equal a human brain. However, even most computer scientists have grown wary of sweeping pronouncements and some feel that any estimates should be made in terms of decades or centuries rather than years.

The dream of conscious machines will never disappear because science has no way of proving it impossible. Besides, people seem to be too enamoured with the idea to give it up. However, not much faith is being placed on it happening in the near future.

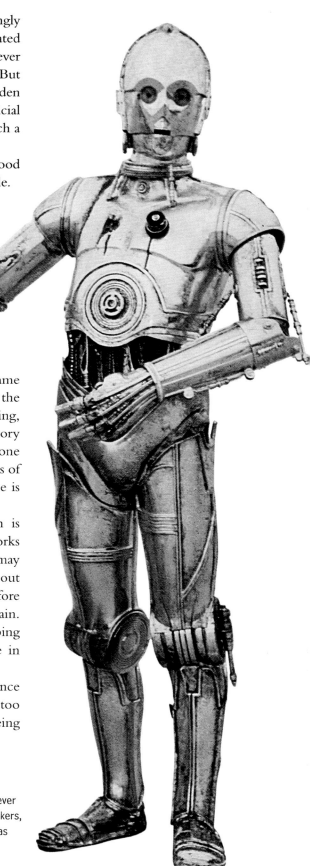

Stranger than fiction The science of artificial intelligence is never far from science fiction. In the imaginations of writers and film makers, robots like *Star Wars'* C3PO are given human characteristics such as reflection, self-awareness and self-interest.

2 STATES OF CONSCIOUSNESS

Have you ever woken to find that the thought 'perhaps I'm just dreaming' occurred to you while you were, indeed, dreaming? Moments like this are when we begin to catch a glimpse of the many-layered, all-pervasive, yet highly changeable nature of consciousness.

A commonsense view of consciousness would seem to say that you must be awake to experience it. Yet did you know that brain activity can be just as busy during sleep? In fact, there are different states of consciousness, and the dividing line between them – and between consciousness and unconsciousness – is by no means hard and fast. Furthermore, we can alter our state of consciousness by various mental and physical means.

Behind all experiences of consciousness lies the mind's remarkable power to construct 'virtual reality' from within. We have all experienced this power in dreams, but even in normal consciousness our thoughts and sensations are to a large extent produced internally by the brain, rather than being direct perceptions of the outside world. This power is the source of illusions and hallucinations – but it is also the gateway to the common reality we share with others.

TYPES OF CONSCIOUSNESS

There is no single 'normal' state of consciousness. Every person experiences a huge range of mental conditions every day as the brain adapts to changing circumstances.

The dividing line between conscious and unconscious states is not sharp. Even within consciousness, there are different degrees. In dreamless sleep you may not be conscious of anything at all, or maybe just of vague thoughts or feelings. When you are daydreaming, you may not be conscious of some of the things in your environment. For example, someone may be talking quite close by and yet you are unaware of it.

A racing driver is acutely conscious of his environment - of the bends in the track, the speed of the car, the position of other cars. But he is probably not very conscious of what is going on in his own mind because he does not have time to notice whether he is feeling afraid or to think about his thoughts. The driver is conscious of his environment but not self-conscious.

Three degrees of awareness

The various states of consciousness can be divided according to the degree of awareness they involve. According to philosopher David Rosenthal from New York, we can describe three main types. The first and most basic state is when we perceive things through our senses, but do not have any thoughts about these perceptions. This happens when you react to, say, a visual stimulus without being consciously aware that you have perceived anything. Think of those times when you carry out familiar routines – driving home from work, for example – without conscious awareness of what you are doing. If something alerts you to your state, you may realise that you have driven through sev-

> **"By introspection we have access only to a limited amount of what is going on in our brain."**
>
> Francis Crick, 1994

Real lives

LOST IN REFLECTION

John S. chose to study philosophy at university because he was intensely interested in his own thought processes. His studies encouraged him to concentrate so hard on them that he eventually became dislocated from ordinary life.

'There was a period of my life when I seemed to be permanently stuck on the introspective level of consciousness. Whenever I saw something, I would barely take it in before I found myself thinking about thinking about it. I would look at a flower, and instead of feeling the pleasure of the sight I would think "I am looking at a flower and thinking that I am finding it pretty". Then I would think "But am I really finding it pretty, or am I just thinking that I think it is pretty?" It became such a habit, this sort of reflection, that I stopped feeling anything directly at all – I seemed to be experiencing everything at second-hand. It was as though I was observing my mental processes through a microscope. It was very alienating, and I started to miss having direct feelings. Or, to be precise, I started to think that I should be missing having direct feelings!

'I trained myself to stop thinking about what I was thinking by doing things that were so terrifying they left no room for thought. I took up parachute jumping, and did a bungee-jump, and learned to ride a horse. I was so absorbed in the physical sensations produced by these activities that there was no room for reflection. Gradually I found I could extend that feeling of total immersion to less terrifying pastimes. I still sometimes lose myself in contemplation of my own thought processes. But I try not to – life is too short.'

eral sets of traffic lights with no memory of their colour. You assume that you noticed the lights because you reacted to them appropriately, but you have no actual memory of it and so cannot be sure. So how did you negotiate the lights safely? The answer is you that reacted quite unconsciously, perceiving the lights without being aware that you were perceiving them. The same unconscious brain mechanisms that allow us to do this also guide our actions in many other activities (see page 70).

The next type of consciousness is the direct awareness of whatever is taking your attention. In this state, you are consciously aware of the contents of your mind – whether these are inner thoughts, such as what to buy for dinner, or more sensory experiences such as trying to walk fast against driving rain. However, you are not reflecting on the thoughts in your mind, so your sense of 'self' is kept in the background. A mountain climber who is completely absorbed in climbing a rock face is intensely conscious in this way. Operating just at this level of awareness, the climber is living in the moment, simply experiencing the flow of the climb and not consciously 'owning' the experience. The loss of self in such 'flow' experiences (and similarly in meditation) appears to produce intense happiness.

Finally, there is the third type known as reflective consciousness, in which you are aware of yourself as having the experience. In this case, you are consciously aware not just of what you are perceiving, but also that it is you perceiving it: your sense of self is brought to the fore. So you do not simply have a thought, you also think about it as though looking at it from outside. We use reflective consciousness in many different ways: in thinking whether we have perceived something correctly or not, or whether we should believe some information, or whether our recall of an event is accurate. This type of consciousness enables us to reflect on our perceptions, beliefs and memories as though they are 'objects' in our minds. Reflective consciousness is also useful in social thinking, such as deciding whether to trust others – or even ourselves – but it can have a downside: thinking too much about what we are doing, such as when giving a talk or making a move in sport, can actually hinder our performance.

 TRY IT YOURSELF

KEEPING A CONSCIOUSNESS DIARY

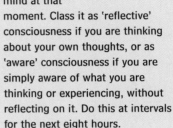

To monitor your own consciousness, set a kitchen timer to ring at intervals of between 30 and 90 minutes. When it rings, note down what is in your mind at that moment. Class it as 'reflective' consciousness if you are thinking about your own thoughts, or as 'aware' consciousness if you are simply aware of what you are thinking or experiencing, without reflecting on it. Do this at intervals for the next eight hours.

Next day, set the timer to ring as before. This time, when it rings, jot down all the thoughts you can recall since it last went off. You will probably find that there are far more introspective thoughts in the recall diary than the one made at the time – an indication of how knowledge of our own consciousness is distorted by memory.

Conscious operations?
We often carry out very familiar routines in a state that is like being on autopilot. Although operating efficiently, we are not consciously aware of what we are doing.

SLEEP AND CONSCIOUSNESS

Every night we shut our eyes, let the mind slip its moorings and enter the blank limbo of sleep. While it is tempting to treat sleep simply as a state of unconsciousness, psychologists tell a very different story in which sleep is really not as far from waking as it first appears.

> **"All men whilst they are awake are in one common world: but each of them, when he is asleep, is in a world of his own."**
>
> Plutarch, Greek biographer, AD 100

Being asleep seems to give us a glimpse of what it would be like to be dead. Sleep undoubtedly appears to extinguish the light of experience, even if our slumber is sometimes fitful or perturbed by the odd dream or nightmare. However, sleep research shows that our repose is a surprisingly active affair in which consciousness is never really switched off.

Brain recordings reveal that we spend each night alternating between two very distinct types of sleep – the deep steady electrical rhythm of slow-wave sleep (SWS) and the frantic buzz of REM sleep (so-called for the rapid eye movements in which the eyeballs seem to chase phantom visions). We begin each night in SWS. At first this is so deep that we are practically comatose. Then, after about

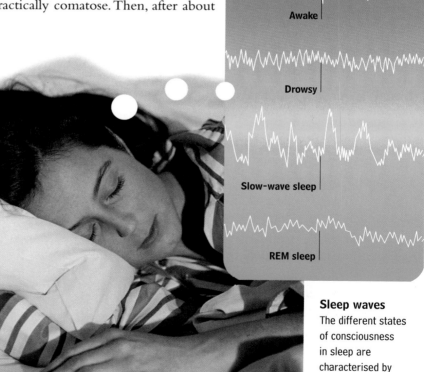

Sleep waves
The different states of consciousness in sleep are characterised by marked changes in the electrical activity of the brain, as shown in this electro-encephalogram (EEG).

FACT FILE

CONSCIOUS ASPECTS OF SLEEP

Looking at mental functioning while awake and in REM sleep yields some interesting comparisons:

• While awake, our thoughts and intentions are generally clear and directed, but in REM sleep they are confused and illogical.

• Perception is strong in both states, although in REM sleep it is directed towards internally generated sensations rather than to the external world.

• Memory also is strong in both states, with more distant memories rather than recent ones typically dominant during REM sleep.

• Instinct is a strong influence in REM sleep, whereas in waking it is mediated by rational thinking.

90 minutes, there comes a brief interruption of REM, which lasts about ten minutes. As the night goes on, the switch-over between SWS and REM continues to occur every 90 minutes or so, but the REM periods get much longer and the SWS periods become progressively shallower. On average, we spend about one quarter of every night in REM sleep.

The dreaming brain

When REM sleep was first discovered in the 1950s, it was thought to be the only sleep phase in which dreams occurred. However, it has since been found that mental activity of a sort goes on all night long. Even subjects roused from SWS usually report vague ruminations. US psychologist David Foulkes describes these slow-wave dreams as drowsy thoughts rather than bright images, and, despite their hazy character, their existence shows that the mind muses to itself all through the long hours from dusk to dawn.

Sleep researchers have concluded that the brain never actually shuts down at night. Brain cells have no 'off' switch, and indeed they must fire a few times each second just to stay alive and healthy. So instead of turning its engines off, a better analogy would be that the brain puts itself into neutral when it enters SWS. It puts a block on incoming sensations, preventing external sights and sounds from troubling the mind, and it suspends short-term memory. The resulting state of consciousness is confused and disjointed and any thoughts or images evaporate just as fast as they form.

In REM sleep, the brain switches into quite a different state. Activity in the brainstem is inhibited, temporarily paralysing the body. This essential safety mechanism ensures that dreams are not acted out physically. Then for some reason, the brain erupts into a succession of vivid internally generated imagery. However, the block remains on short-term memory and so the conscious self cannot really fix on what is going on. In a confused way, it tries to make sense of the random images but it never really catches up with them. And any story it spins is usually quickly forgotten on waking.

Functions of sleep

SWS seems to be essential for growth and maintenance, but the purpose of REM sleep is harder to explain. It has been suggested that REM sleep is simply nature's way of keeping us nearly awake, but out of mischief, until morning. It is possible that vivid dreams – the subject of conjecture for centuries – are merely by-products of a slumbering consciousness.

FOCUS ON

SLEEPWALKING

Most of us know someone who walks or talks in their sleep, but some sleepwalking stories are truly bizarre. One woman packed her dogs into her car and drove 20 miles before waking up; another stumbled off the balcony of her holiday hotel, fell 15 feet and did not wake up until she reached hospital. Our capacity to behave unconsciously while asleep is even recognised in law – a number of individuals have been cleared of attempted rape or murder because they were 'asleep' at the time.

Researchers have found there is a clear difference between ordinary sleepwalking and a more specific REM sleep syndrome. Ordinary sleepwalking happens in deep slow-wave sleep. We come awake enough to act on automatic pilot – to get up and do something routine like go to the toilet, or perhaps even take the car for a midnight spin. However, murders and other violent acts must occur in the high arousal of REM sleep, so the usual REM paralysis, the brainstem block on muscular activity that normally prevents us acting out our dreams, is somehow absent in these cases. On closer examination of such people, doctors often find evidence of a degenerative disorder like Parkinson's disease affecting the brainstem.

ALTERED STATES

Most of the time we take consciousness for granted – it is the transparent window through which we view the world. But sometimes the view changes dramatically, as though the window has become distorted or suddenly been flung open. These seemingly mysterious changes are known as altered states.

The contents of our consciousness change from moment to moment. A sensation gives way to an emotion, then a thought, then perhaps a desire or a stab of pain. While no two experiences are exactly alike, the way in which we experience things tends to remain stable. It is rather like watching a film: the action changes from frame to frame, but the screen itself stays the same and is barely noticed.

Sometimes, though, the background 'screen' on which consciousness plays changes and itself becomes the subject of awareness. The change may be profound, as in the extreme distortions caused by hallucinogenic drugs, trance or religious ecstasy; or it may be spontaneous and subtle – the world simply seems different in some undefinable way.

Peaks and troughs

Some altered states are extraordinarily pleasant, but others can be fearful in their unfamiliarity, accompanied by disordered thoughts and terrifying visions. These profound shifts in consciousness are more common than one might think. For example, more than 80 per cent of Americans report having had a 'peak experience' – a sense of being at one with the universe and detached from their normal selves – at some time in their lives.

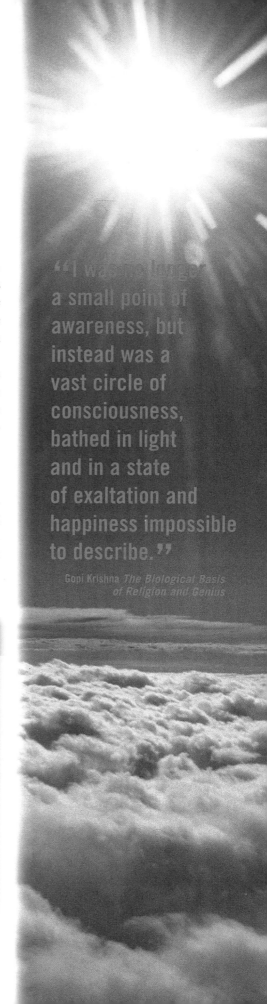

"I was no longer a small point of awareness, but instead was a vast circle of consciousness, bathed in light and in a state of exaltation and happiness impossible to describe."

Gopi Krishna *The Biological Basis of Religion and Genius*

Real lives *A PEAK EXPERIENCE*

Eunice, a 45-year-old advertising executive, has been a churchgoer since having a peak experience.

'I was travelling on business when my car broke down in a strange city. I couldn't get a hotel room, so I asked the emergency repair man if he knew anywhere I could stay. He took me to his own home. His wife showed me to a room, where she had lit a fire in the fireplace. As I watched the flames, they seemed to cast a glow over the room that was far more intense and warm than the fire alone could make it. Then everything was transformed. The room had been tiny, but it seemed to extend into infinity. My gratitude to my hosts became a well of bottomless love for the universe, which seemed to be part of me, not something separate. I recall thinking: "I will never deny the power of the spirit again." Later I found out that this is what people mean by a "peak" experience.'

Peak experiences may happen at any time. One moment the world is a humdrum place; the next it is a glowing universe filled with bliss, beauty and love. People often report being filled with a profound sense of love and gratitude, and ordinary objects and other people seem to radiate beauty. The altered perception may last moments or days, but at the time it seems endless. The person experiencing it is certain that he or she is seeing the world as it really is, and that 'normal' perception is an illusion.

The flip side of peak experience is 'derealisation', in which the normal order of the universe breaks down and the world seems fractured and terrifying. Objects can shrink or become distant; other people seem to be separated by invisible glass shields or vast expanses of space. Individuals experiencing derealisation often report that they feel detached from their own bodies and that their actions seem robotic. Like peak experiences, derealisation can happen at any time – ordinary consciousness suddenly seems uncertain, as though it is a flickering film that may stop at any moment, opening up a chasm of emptiness.

'Recently I had this strange, dreamy feeling for four days without a break,' says Rachel, aged 27. 'I just felt so weird; everything seemed to be far away, voices muffled, and I felt like I was watching myself from the outside. Nothing looked real, I kept forgetting things, staring into space, and all the time this was happening I was thinking "I'm going mad" and trying desperately to get back into my body.' Or as Dale, another regular sufferer from derealisation, explains: 'I see faces, but it is as though I am seeing them in parts – a mouth here, an eyebrow there. I know who they are, but only by piecing the bits together and working it out.'

Fragmented world The experience of 'derealisation' is almost invariably accompanied by an intense feeling of anxiety and restless agitation.

Chemical reality and unreality

Scientists think that altered states occur when different areas of the brain stop interacting in the normal way. Usually, the various information processing systems – sensory, memory, and so on – 'bind' their information to create an integrated perception. However, the integration is not complete – there is always a degree of separation between the components being processed.

A good analogy is to think of a photograph printed in a newspaper. Get too close and all you can see are the individual dots that make up the image: the meaning of the picture is lost. Get too far away and all the picture becomes a blur. In a normal state of consciousness, the picture created by the brain is integrated tightly enough for the individual dots to be invisible, yet it is still close enough to the observer for the whole image to be seen and recognised. A peak experience is like viewing the picture from a great distance – everything seems to be 'one'. In derealisation, the picture is seen too close and so appears fragmented.

The chemistry of consciousness

To create the normal state of consciousness – to allow us to view a complete picture – neurons in different parts of the brain fire in synchrony, and 'pool' their knowledge (see page 19). The synchronisation is mediated by neurochemicals such as dopamine, the so-called 'pleasure chemical'. When levels of dopamine are in the normal range, the emotional processing areas of the limbic system in the brain resonate with parts of the cortex, where memory, thought and perception are located, to unify perceptions. At the same time, other neurotransmitters in the brain inhibit the effect of dopamine; this prevents total synchrony, providing the 'distance' necessary to see the whole picture.

During peak experiences, it seems likely that dopamine, and possibly other chemicals such as serotonin, flood the brain. Activity in the limbic system and frontal lobes becomes hyper-synchronised, producing a feeling of euphoria and seamlessness. In derealisation, it is likely that the opposite happens. Dopamine levels fall, synchrony is lost between various brain areas, and the fragmented activity produces fragmented consciousness.

Causes of altered states

The chemical changes in the brain that cause us to experience altered states may be brought about by extreme psychological or physical stimuli, such as drugs, chanting, dancing, flashing lights and deep meditation. Sometimes, however, the trigger can be more mundane. For example, even small changes in the brain's oxygen balance can affect consciousness. This is why breathing exercises are often used in techniques to induce trance and relaxation. Saturating the brain with oxygen by over-breathing (taking rapid, short breaths) may cause derealisation, while oxygen

▶▶ ▶▶ CUTTING EDGE ▶▶ ▶▶ CUTTING EDGE ▶▶ ▶▶ CUTTING EDGE ▶▶ ▶▶

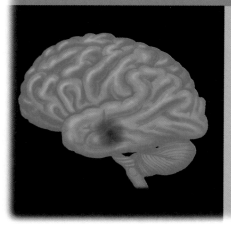

THE 'GOD SPOT'

One of the most impressive types of altered state involves feeling an invisible 'presence' – often interpreted as the awareness of God. Brain studies have found that this feeling comes about due to activity in an area of the temporal lobe. This 'god spot', as it is popularly known, is commonly activated in situations where a period of stress is suddenly brought to an end by a pleasant experience. It can also

be stimulated artificially, or induced by transcranial magnetic stimulation (which inhibits activity in specific parts of the brain). The temporal lobes are one of the areas associated with our sense of self. One theory about the mysterious presence felt when the god spot area is inhibited on one side of the brain, is that the equivalent area on the other side floods consciousness with a ghostly self-sense experienced as coming from outside.

FACT: Measurements of electrical activity at 'acupoints' on the body — the places used in Chinese acupuncture — have found a link between reports of peak experiences and changes in the flow of current.

On a high Falls in oxygen supply can cause unexpected changes in conscious state and can lead to fatal errors of judgment. This sometimes happens to climbers at high altitudes, where the atmosphere is lacking in oxygen.

FOCUS ON

MEDICINES AND THE MIND

Many drugs used to treat illnesses affect the brain in such a way that consciousness is altered. Some drugs are designed to do this: tranquillisers, anti-depressants and some painkillers work directly on the brain, altering the flow of neurotransmitters to improve mood or stem pain. However, the effects of these drugs cannot be precisely predicted. Sometimes they do not just relieve unpleasant symptoms, but produce experiences like derealisation or euphoria. Other drugs also affect the brain indirectly: antihistamines, for example, can produce drowsiness, and steroids may produce euphoria.

depletion may produce the dreamy 'out-of-the-body' state. Oxygen starvation may account for some of the strange near-death experiences reported by individuals who suffer trauma in accidents or during cardiac arrest (see page 120). Less dramatic falls in oxygen may cause a general downgrading of consciousness – a cotton-woolly feeling in the head, and lapses of memory and judgment. This sometimes happens to climbers at high altitudes, where the atmosphere is thin, and on aircraft where cabin pressure is lower than normal.

Sleep deprivation may also bring about alterations in consciousness. In the short term, lack of sleep tends to produce euphoria – a buzzy 'high' that can verge on mania. The effect is so pronounced that sleep deprivation is sometimes used to treat depression. In the long run, however, it causes severe irritability and even hallucinations. The reasons for these effects are not fully understood.

Alterations in body temperature may also affect consciousness. A fever, for example, makes neural tissue more irritable, and may produce random, spontaneous activity in brain cells, which leads to the rushing thoughts and strange impressions known as delirium. The 'aura' felt by epileptics just before they have a seizure is caused by excessive neuronal activity. When this occurs in the temporal lobes, it often produces transcendent feelings similar to those felt during peak experiences.

INDUCING ALTERED STATES

While altered states of consciousness can be frightening or unpleasant experiences, they can also be intensely pleasurable. Some people claim that they can provide glimpses of a deep reality beyond the reach of everyday thought. It is not surprising that people have developed numerous techniques to explore these states.

Everyone deliberately alters their state of consciousness many times a day. Whenever you take a deep breath to calm yourself down or watch a funny film to cheer yourself up, you are using a mind-altering technique. However, these forms of mind manipulation do not produce a radically different quality of consciousness: they merely intensify or blunt it a little. To achieve the states beyond – of ecstasy, or of the 'no-self' oneness with the universe reported by mystics – most people need extraordinary stimuli or must learn how to make their brains function in an unusual way. Every society, in every age, has had its own methods of doing this.

Altered states result from changes in the workings of the brain. These can be elicited in three main ways: by manipulating neuronal activity directly with drugs; by changing brain state using sensory stimuli, such as dance, breathing exercises or other physical rituals; and by using the mind itself to change its own thought patterns through meditation or other psychological techniques. Sometimes different methods are combined to augment the effect.

The Magic Bus Writer Ken Kesey's psychedelic bus is prepared for an event in San Francisco in 1966. A significant part of 1960s culture was inspired by drug-induced altered states.

Drug-induced states

Drugs offer the shortest path to a 'visionary' state. Although many mind-altering substances are illegal, vast numbers of people use them. These include synthetic chemicals like Ecstasy and LSD and natural substances including cannabis and heroin.

Drug-induced pleasure results from changes to chemical pathways in the brain. The 'high' produced by nearly all recreational drugs results from the release, or increased retention, of the 'pleasure' chemical dopamine. Some drugs also affect other neurotransmitters (brain chemicals): serotonin and endorphins promote feelings of serenity; noradrenaline gives a feeling of excitement; and inhibitory neurotransmitters close down some normal brain processes. Drugs that increase noradrenaline (cocaine, amphetamines) create a feeling of energy and power; those that work on serotonin and endorphins (Ecstasy, heroin) may produce a deep glow of warmth; and those that affect the dopamine system (cannabis, magic mushrooms) may intensify or distort sensory perception.

The precise effects that a drug exerts on consciousness depend on which chemical pathways are affected, on how these changes interact with the subject's mood and expectations, and on the context in which the drug is taken. Certain drugs, especially synthetic prescription drugs such as tranquillisers and antidepressants, target specific groups of brain cells and so have fairly predictable effects. Most, though, work more randomly, altering many different chemical pathways, producing complicated and often unpredictable changes. A little alcohol drunk at a party, for example, produces a feeling of mild euphoria, while the same amount at the end of a stressful day may induce relaxation.

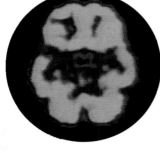

Drug damage Even after four months of abstinence, the brain of a long-term cocaine user (above) shows considerably lower activity compared to a non-user (top). Here, red and yellow indicate the highest levels of brain activity, while blue and mauve show the lowest levels.

Inside the opium den Despite the efforts of the Chinese government to ban them, opium dens flourished in 19th century China.

SPEAKING IN TONGUES

One of the most extraordinary demonstrations of religious ecstasy is 'glossolalia' – speaking in tongues. People affected first become worked up into a state of high excitement, usually as part of a congregation. Then, as though in a trance, they begin to utter sounds in what may seem like a foreign language. Analysis of the sounds shows, however, that they are not words, but strings of repeated noises that lack the structure and variety of true languages. Speaking in tongues was first reported by St Paul at the Church of Corinth in the 1st century and has since cropped up among the French Huguenots in the 17th century, Quakers in the 18th century, Pentecostals in the 19th, and most recently, among charismatic Christians and Mormons.

But drink too much and pleasure may give way to anger, depression or catatonia. Many drugs also have undesirable long-term effects. Ecstasy, for example, can produce 'burn-out' in the neurons it affects, so that users can no longer function normally. The resulting feelings of depression may even lead to a permanent mood disorder.

Dance trance

Altered states can be reached legally, and far more safely, by using sensory or psychological stimuli to change patterns of brain activity. One common technique is dance. Moving the body to a persistent rhythm while shutting out all other thought encourages the release of dopamine in the limbic system, giving a similar effect to certain drugs. Depending on the context and the mental state of the dancer, the result may be heightened awareness of sensory stimuli, which makes the environment seem more vivid and exciting, or a dreamy, euphoric trance.

In the West, dance is primarily a social event. Its cheering effects are more to do with its ability to break down social barriers than to induce altered states. But in other cultures, the purpose of group dance is often spiritual. Shamanic rituals, for example, involve dancing to a repetitive rhythm for hours or sometimes days – long enough for the body to 'know' the music without having to hold it in mind. Movement becomes automatic, leaving the conscious mind free to become aware of messages from the spiritual self. Dancers in this state often experience 'separation' from their bodies and may feel as though they have moved into an alternative reality.

For some people, music alone can produce a similar effect. Most of us have experienced an upwelling of emotion in response to a particularly beautiful or haunting melody. Such a response may be the precursor to feelings of transcendence beyond mere pleasure. Chanting, such as that of Gregorian monks, taps into this channel of experience, with repetitive sounds freeing the mind to tune into spiritual experience.

Ceremony and ritual

Any ritual, even making a cup of tea, calms the mind, because the familiarity of the actions releases consciousness from the task of directing body movements. Some cultures have developed rituals that extend this effect and lead the participants into altered states. The Japanese tea

Ritual dance This Sudanese witch doctor performs a symbolic dance as part of a healing ritual. The repetitive, rhythmic movements of the dance help to induce an altered state of consciousness.

"When I enter a meditative state it is as though the three-dimensional world gives way to one that has many other dimensions."

Shinzen Young, an experienced meditator

The art of ritual Many ceremonies involve purposeful, repetitive actions and movements, which induce altered states of consciousness by quietening the mind and inducing serenity. Chanoyu, the Japanese tea ceremony, developed from Zen Buddhism and combines the four qualities of harmony, respect, cleanliness and tranquillity.

ceremony, for example, is meant to induce relaxation and concentration. Most religious services are deliberately ritualistic and designed to free the mind to take in awareness of God. Some depend on repetitive prayers, actions and sensory stimulation; for example, in Roman Catholicism the 59 beads of the Rosary provide a tactile focus for cycles of prayer. In other traditions, wailing, singing and swaying are encouraged.

The power of thought

Some rituals dispense with physical actions altogether. Instead, the individual goes through a programme of familiar mental behaviours to slow down the frantic rush of thoughts and sensations that typify waking consciousness. This type of practice, known as meditation, takes many forms. It may involve focusing the mind on a thought, an image, a sensation such as breathing, or an imagined sound such as a mantra. The aim of meditation is to rid the mind of content so that only 'pure' awareness remains. It is very difficult to achieve this state because our brains are designed to dart around constantly.

Although meditative states seem to take practitioners outside the everyday mental realm, brain scans show that, like other mind states, they are marked by distinct patterns of brain activity. Compared to brains in a normal state of attentive awareness, the meditating brain has less activity in the sensory cortex – particularly the parietal lobe, which processes information about the body – and it is more active in the parts of the frontal lobes that are concerned with holding attention. Some studies have shown that spiritual experience also activates certain areas of the temporal lobes – the so-called 'god spot' (see page 40).

(see page 40)

Real lives

FINDING THE WAY
Meditation is unlike most endeavours in that the harder you try to do it, the harder it is to achieve, as Abigail discovered.

'I tried and tried to meditate, but nothing happened – I'd dutifully intone my mantra, but all the time I'd be making shopping lists. Then one day I just gave up. It was a group session so I went into the meditative pose and did the breathing exercises. When we stopped twenty minutes later I realised when I opened my eyes that I had been somewhere I had never been before, though I hardly realised it at the time. It was so peaceful, quiet and blissful. I found I had a huge smile on my face that lasted all day. It wasn't that I did anything different – it was what I didn't do that mattered. I didn't try, I didn't worry, I didn't get annoyed that it wasn't working. And that, I realised, is the key – just let go, and it happens.'

HYPNOSIS

Hypnosis is a subject that leaves the experts divided. Some say the trance state produces genuine changes in the brain; others say people are only ever feigning. The truth probably lies in between.

Hypnotism has fascinated people ever since Franz Mesmer wowed 18th-century high society with his displays of control over the minds of others (see pages 68–69). But what is hypnosis? Is it a special level of consciousness, a clever manipulation of normal consciousness, or just quackery? The best answer seems to be that under hypnosis we lose ourselves in vivid imagery and hand over control of this imagery – and so our behaviour – to someone else.

Hypnotic technique

Today's professional hypnotists use a simple conversational technique pioneered in the 1940s by US psychotherapist Milton Erickson. After some small talk to establish a rapport, the hypnotist directs the subject's attention inwards by asking, for example, if his or her hands feel heavy. As the subject becomes absorbed in this thought, the hypnotist starts to assert control, suggesting that one hand is now so light it will rise. Picturing this in mind, some subjects will feel the suggestion to be true and allow their hand to float upwards. The hypnotist can now move on to more elaborate feats of suggestion – such as regressing the person to a past life, or suggesting that an onion is a nice crunchy apple. The person will imagine what the hypnotist asks and respond to the image as if it were authentic.

But is this state of mind real? Studies show that only about one in ten people have mental images so strong they seem like genuine perceptions. For most of us, hypnotic imagery appears fleeting and dull: we cannot shake off the knowledge that the images are 'pro-

An onion a day? People in a hypnotic state have been persuaded to bite into an onion, believing it to be an apple.

FOCUS ON

MINDBENDING SPIES

Recently released CIA files confirm that hypnosis – along with LSD and brain-zapping magnets – was just one of many mind-warping techniques tested out during the Cold War. However, the results were too unreliable to show that hypnotism could be used to force people to do things if they do not want to.

Nonetheless, according to Dr Armen Victorian, author of *Mind Controllers*, the CIA hatched some extraordinary plans. One was to implant a microscopic radio receiver in the ear – or even nostril – of an unsuspecting victim. The idea was that the victim would be cornered and, under hypnosis, have the device inserted, which would then be used for hypnotic control. Later, a whispered radio message could activate them as an assassin, spy or saboteur.

"We are not removing the customer's ability to say no. We are simply increasing their ability to say yes."

Robert Farago, professional hypnotist defending hypnotism courses for car salespeople

duced'. But if we are dragged up on stage, or have paid money to a hypnotherapist, we may feign simply out of embarrassment.

Experiments also show that motivation techniques can match the effect of a supposed hypnotic state. In one test, men were asked to hold a brick at arm's length for as long as they could. Unhypnotised, they lasted barely five minutes; hypnotised, they could stretch to 15 or 20. However, when unhypnotised men were told that women usually managed 20 minutes, suddenly the men found that they could last this long as well.

The 'hidden observer'

One intriguing phenomenon seems to provide evidence on both sides. In a typical study, strongly hypnotised subjects were first told that a small part of their mind – the 'hidden observer' – would always know what was going on during the session. Still under hypnosis, they were given lists of words – along with the suggestion that certain words on the list were not actually there. The subjects duly swore that the words were indeed missing from the lists. But when their 'hidden observer' was addressed, they reported being able to see the 'missing' words after all.

Some researchers say this means that there was always at least a part of the subject's mind that was behaving normally, quite unhypnotised. Others, however, argue that because hypnosis can divide consciousness in this way, with one part of the mind apparently having access to information denied to another part, the hidden observer effect shows that hypnosis involves a real state of dissociation. More recently, brain scanning machines have been used to examine some of the 10 per cent who do have super-strength mental imagery, and it was found that hypnosis could induce a visible change in their brain state. For example, when hypnotised to see a black and white picture as coloured, the scans suggested the subjects really did paint in the sensory impressions of colour. So while hypnosis is a largely self-induced state rather than a helpless trance, some people do have the mental imagery to make it a powerful experience.

Colourful fantasies People strongly suggestible to hypnosis can often be led to see colour in black and white images.

Real lives SURGERY WITHOUT ANAESTHETIC

To prove the power of hypnosis, 58-year-old Bernadine Coady decided to use it as her only anaesthetic during a lengthy operation to reconstruct a misshapen foot. When her hypnotist failed to show up for the operation, she went ahead and hypnotised herself.

Ahmed Shair, surgeon at the Fitzwilliam Hospital in Cambridgeshire, admitted that he felt unusually tentative as his scalpel was poised to make the first incision. The operation involved cutting through muscle and even bone to lengthen some tendons. But Mrs Coady coped by imagining her leg to be an unfeeling iron rod. She turned the waves of pain into ocean waves crashing vainly against a sea wall.

The surgeon said afterwards: 'I have heard of this sort of thing happening but never believed it. When we sawed through the bone she took herself deeper into sleep. She was in absolute control.'

WAYS TO EXPERIENCE ALTERED STATES

Our normal state of consciousness is constructed on the basis of our expectations, which make the world around us a consistent and familiar place. It can be an interesting experiment to try shaking up your expectations deliberately, and through this to induce an alteration in your mental state. The approaches described here will not take you into a kaleidoscopic world of psychedelia, but they can generate subtle and intriguing alterations of consciousness.

ENTERING THE FLOW

Try this exercise the next time you go for a walk. While walking, look straight ahead, but pay attention to your peripheral vision. If you're on a path, pay attention to what lies on either side of the path (such as hedges), rather than the path itself. Stretch your attention as wide as you can – the fields beyond the hedges, for example. Become aware of your other senses – hearing, smell, skin touch and pressure. Soon, you will feel that everything flows more than usual, and you are part of the flow. Your walking is only one action among all the movements in your vicinity; your awareness is part of the awareness that creatures around you are experiencing. Continue until there is only the flow; only the pulse of the world.

LIGHT-HEADEDNESS

In his book *Walden,* Henry Thoreau describes how he induced a dissociated state of consciousness by simply gazing at the reflection of the sun on Walden pond. You can try this for yourself. On a sunny day, sit or lie by a calm lake and watch the reflection of the sun on the surface of the water. Ensure that you won't be disturbed – maybe try this exercise with a friend, taking turns. Just keep gazing, without distraction. Don't hold onto particular thoughts in your mind – allow your attention to drift where it will, but keep your gaze fixed. After a while, you should find yourself moving into a state of consciousness subtly altered from normality. An alternative method of entering this state is to gaze at a bright light reflected in a crystal.

SENSORY DEPRIVATION

To see how your mind responds to a diminishing of sensation, try this route to temporary sensory deprivation. This is not so much a matter of depriving the senses of any input, but of removing any formed, meaningful input. The ideal is to use a flotation tank, since the environment can be carefully controlled. If you have no access to one, you can create similar conditions in your own home. Use a bed in a warm room with dim lighting. Cover your eyes with a bubble wrap mask (you are not trying to blindfold yourself, merely creating a diffuse light). De-tune a radio so you hear a hissing noise and listen to it through headphones. These provide the basics for sensory deprivation, Choose a time of day when you are feeling fairly alert – the object is to stay awake. Try to ensure that there is no air movement or strong smells in the room. Lie down and relax with your eyes open under the mask and the hissing in your ears, and see what happens.

WILD IMAGININGS

The French poet Rimbaud recommended a 'long, tremendous and methodical disturbance' of perceptions and their interpretations in the mind as a way of experiencing an altered state of consciousness. See if you can follow his method. Deliberately imagine that an object that you are seeing is something other than what it is. If it's a book, imagine it's a block of wood; if it's a cat, see it as a mutant fox. So too with sound: label the rustling of leaves as the sound of an animal; the voice of someone in the room as a radio voice. This exercise is hard to start with, and may not be something that you take to, but the method gets easier with practice. Don't worry if it sounds bizarre – that's the point!

CHANGING NAMES

Your name is a key part of your identity. As soon as you hear your name, a host of changes occur in your conscious mind – you pay attention, you become alert, you start questioning what is going on. You will realise how much of your conscious world is centred on your name if you change it. Unless you want to experience a serious sense of dislocation, a total change is not recommended. However, you could make arrangements within a group of close friends. The 'alias' that you choose may reflect aspects of your personality, which may be worth analysing (most people entering internet chat rooms use aliases, which are often revealing). Agree that you will be called by your alias for the course of a weekend. You will discover how de-centred you can become.

TRANCE DANCE

Total absorption in a physical activity can transport you to a trance-like state. You can try this with a group of friends. Clear your biggest room to make a dance-floor. Make sure there is nothing to trip over and that everyone has enough space to turn a full circle with arms outstretched, without touching anyone else. Then – with the exception of one or two trustworthy supervisors – everyone should put on a blindfold and dance for at least 30 minutes. The hypnotic rhythms of African tribal music are particularly good for this exercise. Let the music take over, clear your mind and just let yourself go. To reground yourself afterwards, lie down quietly for 20 minutes.

THE MIND'S VIRTUAL REALITY

The world of our experiences owes as much to our minds as to the world outside. All our experiences – sights, sounds, smells and tastes – are our mind's interpretations of the physical reality that exists around us. Without a mind to perceive it, a sound is just a pattern of vibration in the air. So our perceptions are all in essence an elaborate form of 'virtual reality'.

> **"The mind is the real instrument of sight and observation."**
>
> Pliny the Elder, 1st century AD

Imagine that you have landed on a strange planet. You leave your spacecraft but are unable to make out anything at all; you feel nothing, see nothing, hear nothing. Back inside your craft you consult your instruments and discover that there is, in fact, a rich diversity of matter and energy criss-crossing this new world. There are electromagnetic waves, vibrations and molecules – it is just that they are so different from those on Earth that your body has not evolved to be sensitive to them. They are like the high-pitched sound waves that bats use to communicate or the infra-red light-waves that can be seen by night-owls.

Consulting technical manuals on board, you design a suit that can detect these alien forces. You build in sensors to pick up the vibrations, cells that respond to the electromagnetic waves, and receptors for the molecules that are carried around in the planet's atmosphere. Then you make a transducer that turns the

THINK AGAIN!   THE REALM OF OUR SENSES

Our sensory system has evolved to pick up the type of information that is most useful for our survival. We can see light only in a small part of the electromagnetic spectrum. However, this part includes the wavelengths of light that certain key chemicals in our bodies and environment reflect. For example, haemoglobin and chlorophyll reflect in this range – so we see blood as bright red and plants as bright green. Similarly, the sounds we hear come from a narrow range of vibrational frequencies, so we cannot hear the shrill echolocatory signals of bats, for example – but these are of no benefit or threat to us. If we could redesign our sense organs so that they picked up a different range of stimuli, the world would be very different. We would see different colours, smell many more smells, and hear things that we are usually deaf to.

A world without red Some people's vision is abnormal because the retinal cells are insensitive to red, green or blue. The top picture shows what these red tulips might look like to someone without red vision. Not only are colours changed, but the relative contrasts are different – the blue flowers stand out far more than the red.

TWO-WAY PROCESSING

Conscious perceptions of the outside world are produced in the brain via a combination of bottom-up and top-down processing. Raw visual data from the eyes is sent to an area of the brain at the back of the opposite hemisphere, where 'bottom-up' processing begins. This continues as the perceptual information travels forward, with meaning added at each stage. Meanwhile, conceptual information (such as memories, expectations and verbal labels) is constantly fed back from frontal brain areas. This 'top-down' process integrates the perception into the existing conceptual framework and brings it to consciousness. The final perceptual experience is thus unique to each individual.

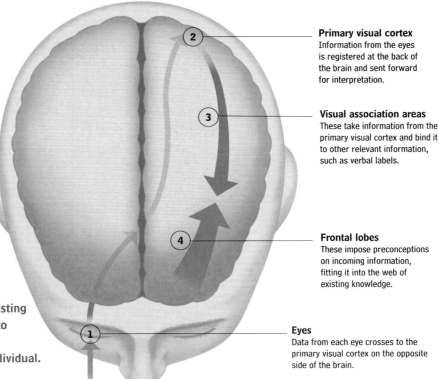

Primary visual cortex
Information from the eyes is registered at the back of the brain and sent forward for interpretation.

Visual association areas
These take information from the primary visual cortex and bind it to other relevant information, such as verbal labels.

Frontal lobes
These impose preconceptions on incoming information, fitting it into the web of existing knowledge.

Eyes
Data from each eye crosses to the primary visual cortex on the opposite side of the brain.

suit's responses into stimuli that your body can understand. Wrapped in the suit, you step out again into your new world. This time it is a place filled with objects and resonating with sound, colour, taste, smell and touch.

Our bodies are like that spacesuit. Just as the alien world can only be perceived when we equip ourselves with appropriate sensors, so our own world comes into existence only when its energy forms are translated by the brain and our nervous system into experience. What we think is a view of something 'out there' is in fact a sensation created by the brain from the messages received through the sense organs. In this sense, it is not so much reality itself as 'virtual reality'. The reason why we all perceive the world so similarly is that we all have similar nervous systems – we are all wearing the same type of spacesuit. But how do our brains create conscious experiences from the patterns of energy in the environment?

Constructing experience

A perceptual experience – such as seeing an object, hearing a sound or feeling a texture – occurs when matter or energy in the outside world stimulate our sense organs. For example, when we see something it is because light rays of the correct frequency hit the retina, which then sends signals via the optic nerve to the visual cortex at the back of the brain. Here the information is decoded and turned into a raw sensation. From here, the information passes to the frontal lobes, where it is interpreted conceptually and becomes a conscious visual experience, identified as a familiar – or unfamiliar – object.

HOW TO.... ?

THINK YOURSELF FIT

When you imagine moving your body, the 'body map' you carry in your brain springs into action, producing the sensation of movement even if you remain perfectly still. The brain still sends signals that try to activate muscles around the body, and although large movements are inhibited, the muscles nevertheless contract in preparation for the movement. This means you can increase muscle tone in the same way (though not to the same degree) as really carrying out the movement.

☞ TRY IT YOURSELF   THE LIMITS OF IMAGINATION

When you imagine an object or an event, it may at first seem just as clear and detailed as 'real' experience. But if you test it out, you will usually find the imagined experience is full of gaps and indistinct: its clarity is an illusion.

You can try this by summoning up a familiar image – some patterned curtains in your house, say. Close your eyes and concentrate on one particular part of the image – the pattern near the top, for example. When you have fixed the image clearly in your mind, zoom in on one part of the pattern – say, a flower. Can you see its form in detail?

Can you even state exactly what colours are in it? When you try to capture these details, the haziness of the image becomes apparent – very few people can visualise all the details. This may be because imagination depends more on top-down processing, whereas externally generated images are produced by proportionately more bottom-up activity. Both give the subjective impression of dense sensation, so the experience is very similar. But the actual amount of sensory information contained in imagined experience is relatively sparse – our brains 'fill in' the missing bits.

However, the flow of information is not exclusively from the sensory to the conceptual areas of the brain: the neural pathways run in both directions. When we imagine an experience or call up an image from memory, the flow is reversed. Activity in the frontal region of the brain generates a concept, which passes to the sensory cortices and prompts them to produce appropriate sensory signals. These are then fed forward again, where they are experienced as sensory events rather than just as abstract concepts. En route, they may trigger activity in the limbic system, producing emotions as well. The more the sensory cortex is stimulated, the more vivid the recollection – so imaginary sights may vary from vague impressions to hallucinations so real as to be indistinguishable from the real events.

FACT: The sensory nerves of the body can be trained to 'see', much as the eye does. If electrodes are attached to the skin, and then used to send pulses of electricity that represent the shape of objects, the brain learns to interpret the signals as vision. Using this method, blind people are able to navigate a maze.

For example, if you think of a concept such as 'going swimming tomorrow', the frontal region of the brain stimulates the sensory cortex to produce the neural activity that would normally occur when the body was immersed in water. It may also produce the sort of activity in the visual cortex that would normally be triggered by the sight of water – perhaps a swimming pool or the sea. The image may be very crude – just an impression of water – or highly embellished to include the people you expect to be swimming with, the beach you will be visiting, the feeling of the sun on your skin, the swimming costume you intend to wear. In addition, the thought may trigger dopamine release in the limbic system, which provides a frisson of pleasure – just as though you were experiencing your swimming trip for real.

Time to daydream The fantasies we weave when daydreaming are most easily summoned when we have few distractions. Although they can be very vivid, these inwardly created perceptions are rarely as detailed as ones that we actually experience.

The power of imagination

The detail and vividness of our imagined or remembered imagery depends largely on our ability to focus attention – that is, to limit our brain's activity to the imaginative process. Because many areas of the brain are involved in creating an imagined scenario, any competing cognitive activity will divert resources away from the task. In order to daydream successfully, you must clear your mind of other things and attend to it – just as you have to attend to significant things in the 'real' world.

Internally generated experiences are rarely as rich as those created by outside stimuli because, for very good reasons, the brain is designed to give primary attention to the outside world. If daydreams were as tangible as 'real' experience then we might well fail to notice things that may pose a physical threat, or we might respond physically to events in our own imaginations. So the sensory activity associated with daydreams is easily interrupted by signals coming in from outside: if you are visualising a sunny beach, for example, the image will be shattered if your eye detects a big object moving towards you. This is why daydreaming is difficult in a busy, exciting environment – but seductively easy when there are few distractions.

Real lives SENSORY DEPRIVATION AND HEIGHTENED IMAGINATION

Imagined scenarios tend to be more vivid when there are no outside stimuli to compete with the internally generated sensations. Alice, 20, found this when she experimented with a session in a sensory deprivation tank.

'At first I just felt strange and disoriented. There was nothing to fix on, not even the feeling of heat or cool, or where my limbs were, because they were floating in this blood temperature water. But as I relaxed, images started to swim up in front of my eyes. They were much clearer and more detailed than the sights I can usually conjure up. One of them was a girl's face – not a familiar one – and I could actually count her eyelashes and see the pores on her skin. Later I imagined riding my horse, and found that I could actually feel the motion and the slight friction of my seat in the saddle. I've tried to do this since, by shutting my eyes and concentrating – but it is never as clear.'

VISIONS AND HALLUCINATIONS

Many people have experienced false perceptions. They may have heard phantom footsteps on a dark night, felt a touch on their shoulder when they were alone, or glimpsed a figure in an empty corner of a shadowy room. When these experiences are mistaken for reality, they are known as hallucinations.

There is nothing mysterious about hallucinations. They arise from the same brain machinery that is used when we summon up an image from memory or create a new experience from our imagination. In all these cases, the brain produces sensory experiences in the absence of outside stimuli. These 'false' experiences are usually less vivid than those triggered by external stimuli, so we know that they are not 'real'. But in certain circumstances the imagined experiences can be extremely intense, and we lose our ability to perceive them for what they are.

Seeing what you expect to see

There are two types of hallucinations: those produced spontaneously by a normal brain and those triggered by drugs or by disturbances in brain function. Spontaneous hallucinations are created (like all imaginary experience) from memory. A hallucination can be a discrete 'chunk' of memory, such as a familiar face, or it can be assembled from many 'bits' of past experience spliced together to form something apparently new. The sensory component of the hallucination – what is actually seen, heard or felt – is generated by activity in the sensory cortices, just like ordinary perceptions. But the interpretation of this activity also depends on how the sensations are processed by the parts of the brain that deal with beliefs and expectations. So if two observers both see a black shape in the corner of a room, depending on their expectations one might see a coat on a hook, while the other sees a ghostly figure lurking in the shadows.

Ordinary perceptions, too, are open to different interpretations by different observers. But because they are triggered by external stimuli, the 'real' sensory information tends to override the internal imagery generated by expectation and belief. Someone looking at a picture of a cat when she is expecting a picture of a dog, may 'see' a dog if she takes only a brief glimpse. But the longer she looks at the picture, the harder it is to

Ghosts in the shadows Apparitions with a ghostly quality are common because the sensory apparatus for making out forms in semi-darkness is especially sensitive. This is probably because such an adaptation would once have been useful to our forebears, helping them to detect potential physical threats in the dark.

FOCUS ON

THE SLEEP-WAKE BOUNDARY

Hallucinatory phenomena are often experienced in the twilight state between waking and sleep. These experiences are described as hypnagogic (if they occur as we are falling asleep) or hypnopompic (if they occur as we are waking up).

Hypnagogic hallucinations tend to be visual and often rather alluring. People often report beautiful, dynamic images such as roses unfurling their petals, fascinating landscapes with changing cloud shapes, or colours and kaleidoscopic forms that appear to dance and shimmer.

Hypnopompic phenomena are also primarily visual, but seem to be experienced more fully. People are often convinced that they are awake and therefore find the hallucinations powerful and even frightening. Dreamers may believe that there is an intruder in the room poised to attack them, or that strange creatures are lurking in the darkness. The dreamers may feel even more vulnerable because they are unable to move. This sleep paralysis is a normal feature of REM sleep, and prevents us from acting out our dreams.

sustain the mistaken perception. In other words, the 'bottom-up' content from the senses overrides the signals flowing 'top-down' from the expectations in the conscious brain. Hallucinations, by contrast, contain more 'top-down' content and have little or no outside information to conflict with the self-generated image. For this reason, hallucinations tend, more than ordinary perceptions, to reflect what the mind expects to find.

So people who believe in ghosts are more likely to see them than those who do not. Seeing a dark shadow in a room, they are more likely to notice it, turn their attention to it, and amplify the impression into something that seems very real. By contrast, someone who does not believe in ghosts is unlikely to notice the shadow, and may not even remember seeing it. Similarly, religious believers who expect to see manifestations of gods or saints quite often do. Their visions are wishful embellishments of real perceptions, turning a pattern of currants in a bun into a portrait of Mother Theresa or a cloud formation into an image of the Virgin Mary.

FACT: The Russian composer Dmitri Shostakovitch heard melody hallucinations every time he put his head to one side. He incorporated some of these melodies into his work.

The importance of belief and expectation in shaping visions and hallucinations becomes clear when you compare reports from different cultures. Visions of the Virgin Mary are often reported in Catholic countries, whereas in the USA, where sci-fi movies are a significant influence, sightings of UFOs and aliens are far more common.

Errors of perception

Certain environmental factors predispose us to hallucinations. Many visions occur in semi-darkness because the sensory cells in the eye that detect forms in poor light lie at the periphery of our visual field. This means that when we see objects in the dark, we see them indistinctly – out

'The Nightmare' Henry Fuseli's 1781 painting depicts the demonic figure of an incubus, representing the frightening images experienced in bad dreams. Both nightmares and normal dreams occur during REM sleep, our consciousness producing both terrifying and pleasurable dream narratives.

of the 'corner of the eye'. Darkness also promotes fear, which tends to make our senses more alert. So in scary situations, the visual cortex is more likely to pick up small stimuli that might otherwise be ignored.

We all experience false perceptions from time to time. Usually the error is detected because it does not tally with information from our sense organs or because it does not fit into our belief system. But in some cases, the false perception does tally with our belief system and therefore becomes fixed. Such full-blown hallucinations can be dangerous. For example, an aircraft pilot may misread the position of a needle on a dial, but because the information seems reasonable, he may not examine it closely. Such errors become more common if the pilot is tired or in a situation where information from outside is sparse (when flying through cloud, for example) and they sometimes cause serious accidents.

Dreamscapes

The most familiar way in which our minds produce vivid images and experience without input from the outside world is in dreams. Dreams are the result of activity in the sensory areas at the back of the brain. These become active and produce a stream of sensations, which are woven into a narrative. When we dream, the frontal areas of the brain, which in the waking state select and direct sensory attention according to our wishes, are partially 'turned off'. This means that we have very little control over the content of our dreams – we cannot direct the action in the same way we can in imaginative daydreams.

The frontal areas of the brain are also partly responsible for producing the background sense of self – the awareness of who and where we really are. Because they are underactive in sleep (except in lucid dreaming, see page 58) we are not even aware that we are dreaming, so heightening the reality of the experience.

Hallucination and the damaged mind

People with damaged or diseased brains can suffer severe hallucinations that cannot be distinguished from perceptions triggered by outside stimuli. For example, if a stroke damages the sensory areas of the brain, the

> **"In the dream, I raised my arms and began to rise. I rose through black sky that blended to indigo, to deep purple, to lavender, to white, then to a very bright light. All the time I was being lifted there was the most beautiful music I have ever heard."**
>
> Andy, of Bay City, Michigan

Real lives *VISIONS IN MINIATURE*

Doreen has a severe visual impairment, which makes the real world a blur. Yet she sees imagined perceptions as perfectly concrete, clear and vivid.

'One day I watched an entire circus. The clowns came on, then acrobats, then jugglers – I could see every detail of their costumes; the strings of the balloons held by the clowns, the wires that the acrobats performed on. It went on for hours and it was charming and engrossing. What was really strange about it, though, was that it was all in miniature. The entire Big Top was about the size of my thumbnail.'

FOCUS ON   DRUGS AND HALLUCINATIONS

Hallucinations can be generated by a wide range of drugs. Some, including LSD, peyote, mescal and heroin, are used specifically for this purpose, while others may produce hallucinations as side-effects. These include prescription medicines used to treat high blood pressure (clonidine), pain (pentazocine, fentanyl) and depression (Prozac).

The type of hallucination depends on which part of the brain is most affected by the drug. Those that target the visual cortex produce whirling colours, patterns, and altered perception of the size and shape of objects. Those that affect 'higher' brain areas – where sensations are interpreted – may make objects do peculiar things: a spider may suddenly start doing leapfrog with the cat. Drugs that affect the auditory cortex can alter the way that sound is heard, or generate phantom sounds. Some chemicals (including alcohol and steroids) produce tactile sensations such as the feeling of 'bugs' crawling over the skin. Amyl nitrate produces genital sensations that often induce sexual arousal. Drugs that work mainly on the limbic system, such as Ecstasy, may produce emotional hallucinations such as a heightened sense of beauty and love; and those that excite the frontal lobes (amphetamines, cocaine) generate delusions of power and strength.

'Easy Rider' Very much a product of its time, the 1969 cult movie starring Peter Fonda and Dennis Hopper was notorious for the scenes featuring the characters hallucinating on LSD.

reduced sensory information received from outside is constantly over-ridden by 'top-down' processing, so imagined events appear real. Providing the sufferer's thinking is still normal – that is, if the parts of the prefrontal cortex that govern reason and logical thought are still intact, the odd, imagined material will be recognised as false.

It is when damaged sensory brain function is combined with a bizarre belief system or disordered thinking that false perceptions may be really catastrophic. This occurs in people suffering from disorders such as Alzheimer's disease, schizophrenia and severe depression. For example, some forms of schizophrenia are marked by odd and often terrifying hallucinations that make it impossible for sufferers to function in the real world. The most common form of schizophrenic hallucination is auditory – voices, which may be threatening or dictatorial. In extreme cases, the voices may tell the person to commit suicide or murder.

Brain scans of schizophrenics hallucinating voices show that their auditory cortex is activated in just the same way as when voices are actually heard. They also show that the voices are generated by the speech centres of the person's own brain; and sensors that pick up minute movements of the throat muscles reveal that the person even starts the process of articulating them. When normal people generate silent speech, a signal is sent to the auditory cortex to tell it that the speech comes from 'inside', so the person knows that it is imaginary. In schizophrenics, these signals are absent, so they cannot distinguish between imaginary internal speech and actual voices.

FACT FILE

HALLUCINATIONS

• Visual hallucinations affect about 3 per cent of people with sight problems.

• Sleep deprivation produces hallucinations in most people within 48 hours.

• Phantom limbs, in which amputees experience the presence of missing limbs, are a type of tactile hallucination.

• Artists such as Poe, Coleridge, and Baudelaire used hashish and opiates to increase the richness of their visual imagery.

• One of the constituents of cannabis, dronabinol, produces hallucinations in 5 per cent of people who take it.

Lucid dreaming

The world we enter in our dreams is as vivid and eventful as waking reality. Normally, we have no conscious influence on our dream imagery – we are passive observers. But in lucid dreaming, people can control their dream experiences.

When you dream, your brain's conscious 'control centre' shuts down, and you can no longer direct the focus of your attention or rationally examine your perceptions. This means that you accept your dream experiences, no matter how bizarre, as being completely normal. In lucid dreaming, this changes. The brain's control centre 'wakes up' and restores the sense of self. This allows you to direct your dream narratives as you choose. Experienced lucid dreamers do extraordinary things in their dreams. They can fly, chat to long-lost friends, sunbathe on a sunny beach or eat an exquisite meal.

In a lucid dream, you move into a rich dreamscape – seemingly as real as anything experienced in waking life, but with the freedom of being unconstrained by normal physical laws. The key is that you are able to recognise the dream as illusion. For example, you might dream that a lion is chasing you. Becoming lucid, you realise that you are dreaming, and your fear subsides as you remember that you can control what happens. You can turn the lion into a fluffy toy or make it roll over and ask for its tummy to be tickled. Or you can continue the chase just for the thrill of it.

Lucid dreams can occur spontaneously, but many people can train themselves to have lucid dreams by using visualisation techniques (see opposite).

Therapeutic lucid dreaming

Lucid dreaming is not just entertaining – it can be therapeutic. People can overcome phobias, for example, by confronting and controlling them in lucid dreams. Some psychotherapists believe that significant dream symbols can be interrogated in these dreams, providing insights into unconscious motivations.

HOW TO BECOME A LUCID DREAMER

Lucid dreaming is not a particularly 'natural' state because normal brain chemistry tends to produce either sleep (and dreaming) or wakefulness – not a mixture of the two. However, there is no evidence to suggest that training yourself to enter this state has any adverse effects. The following steps, followed every night, should produce lucid dreaming within weeks or months.

1 Go to bed an hour or so earlier than usual, or have a lie-in. Alternatively, set an alarm a couple of hours earlier than usual, get up when it goes off, then return to bed later for a nap. Lucid dreams tend to occur after one has had the normal dose of ordinary REM sleep.

2 In the hours before bedtime, think hard and repeatedly: 'I will have a lucid dream tonight'. The thought will help to 'prime' the brain for lucidity.

3 Select a 'cue' or 'dreamsign' that your brain will recognise when it occurs in a normal dream. Decide that when the dreamsign appears, you will 'know' that you are dreaming. For example, decide that whenever a red object appears in a dream, your brain will latch on to it and recall that this is a dream.

4 Make an effort to become more aware of your ordinary dreams. Keep a notebook by your bed and, on waking, write down everything you can remember. Make a particular note of objects that seem to appear often and select them as dreamsigns.

5 The moment you have a glimmering of awareness in a dream – the thought 'this is too odd to be real' for instance – zoom in on it rather than letting it drift away. This type of awareness is the gateway to lucidity. Most people experience it fleetingly during normal dreams: the trick is to hold on to the thought and elevate it into consciousness without waking up altogether.

6 When lucidity dawns, relax into it. Do not get excited or try to alter the dreamscape immediately. Just relax and enjoy the scenery. Once you have latched on to the thought that you are dreaming, you will find that lucidity floods in. It feels like waking up – except that, instead of becoming sensorily aware of the outside world, your knowledge is purely conceptual. You 'know' you are in bed, because you remember going to sleep, but you don't actually feel the bed. The sights, sounds and feelings you were experiencing when you were ordinarily dreaming continue unchanged – it is just that now you know they are hallucinations.

7 Test the dream. Sometimes it can be quite difficult to distinguish a lucid dream from wakefulness. One way to test it is to try switching on any type of electrical apparatus – in lucid dreams, there is always a delay between throwing the switch and the device coming to life. And electric lights are always very dim in lucid dreams.

8 Slowly start to control the dream. Decide, for example, to change the weather, or the wallpaper of the room you are in. All you need to do is to have the thought 'let it be sunny', or 'walls turn blue'. If you want to conjure up a person, think about seeing them appear, then turn away from the place where you want to see them. When you turn back they will probably be there. If you want to fly, imagine yourself lifting up very gently – when you feel yourself go, do not try to 'help', just let it happen.

9 If you feel yourself waking up and don't want to, try spinning your dream body around in a circle – it helps to maintain the dreamscape.

10 Never panic. Lucid dreams occasionally produce unpleasant experiences, such as a feeling of a charged atmosphere or a sinister presence. And 'false awakenings' are common – you think you have properly woken up, but find that you cannot move. This is because you are still in sleep paralysis. Fighting against the feeling is pointless and may make you feel as though you are suffocating. Instead, relax, remind yourself that this is a false awakening, and float back into your dreamworld.

PERCEPTION AND REALITY

Perception is more than just seeing. Our personal version of reality comes both from the raw material we pick up from our senses and from the beliefs, desires, memories and expectations that we use to interpret this material. For this reason, the way two individuals experience the world may be very different.

Real lives

EROTOMANIA

Erotomania is a curious type of delusion in which people believe that a person they idolise returns their feelings. Jacob – now receiving counselling after being accused of stalking Elisabeth – recalls how he misread her behaviour.

'Elisabeth worked in my office. I was much too shy to talk to her and I realise now that she probably didn't even know I existed until I started to follow her home and generally make a nuisance of myself. But I got the idea into my head that she had fallen in love with me, as I had with her. I would watch her from a distance, and think that she was sending me signals. She had this habit of flicking her hair back, and every time she did it I thought she was flirting with me. Once I got in her way and she said "watch it!" to me. I took this to mean "watch what I signal to you" – it really thrilled me! Of course I realise now that it was all madness – she didn't even know I was looking, let alone that I thought she was sending me messages. But it all seemed obvious at the time – there was no other way of seeing it.'

Most people have much the same sort of sensory equipment; their eyes, ears and other senses work according to the same physical principles, and the sensory pathways in their brains are wired in similar ways. So if two individuals witness the same event, the raw information that they take in will be more or less the same. But no two people will interpret this information in exactly the same way. Those who share a common culture, background and education are most likely to arrive at similar conclusions, but others may form widely variant pictures.

Perceptions can differ on a number of levels, from the purely sensory to the psychologically complex. For example, imagine that you are presented with a neutral tactile sensation, such as a vibration: if you expect it to be painful, you are likely to perceive it as such; but if you are told beforehand that the vibration will be pleasant, then you will probably experience it as pleasant. Similarly, different people's interpretation of a neutral visual stimulus, such as an irregularly shaped inkblot, can vary considerably. At a more complex level, we all interpret other people's behaviour according to the notions we already hold about those people. For example, if someone you know and like ignores you in the street, you will probably assume that they were simply lost in thought and did not see you passing. But if you dislike that person, you may see their action as a deliberate snub.

Cultural distortions

Prejudices like this pervade our every perception. Sometimes the prejudice is individual, but often it is shared by an entire culture. Take our ideas of beauty. Certain qualities are perceived as beautiful by almost everyone because the human brain is wired to see them as such. For example, every known

Revealing character The Rorschach inkblot test, used by psychologists to assess personality, exploits our tendency to read meaning into an arbitrary pattern. One person may look at this pattern and see two lovers in an embrace, while another might interpret it as two adversaries locked in combat. The difference depends not on information received through the senses, but on how information is interpreted by memory and other 'higher' cognitive functions.

culture values facial symmetry, probably because it indicates health. But other concepts of beauty are clearly determined by culture: in the West, the 'ideal' female form is slim, but elsewhere a slender build indicates weakness or poverty, and an attractive woman is one with the sort of padding that sends well-heeled Westerners rushing to slimming clinics.

Theory of mind

Everyone's perceptions are private. But in order to communicate and share understanding, we must have some idea of the world that other people construct in their minds. Not surprisingly, humans have evolved sophisticated mechanisms for knowing how other people see things. One such mechanism is actually programmed into the human brain: psychologists call it the theory of mind.

Around the age of four years, normal children suddenly develop the ability to know intuitively that other people have a different point of view to their own. The emergence of this skill can be detected by a test in which the child is invited to watch a play acted out by a couple of dolls,

Points of view Two people can take in the same information, but create quite different perceptions from that information. Here, the painters J.M.W. Turner (1775–1851), left, and Canaletto (1697–1768) offer strikingly different interpretations of the same scene – the Grand Canal in Venice.

(F)ocus on *INEVITABLE ILLUSIONS*

There are certain things that we cannot see as they really are – our brains are 'hard-wired' to distort them. Such inevitable illusions include the mask illustrated here. The brain sees a face as convex, not concave. The picture of the mask on the far right is in fact a concave shape – the inside surface of the mask. But the brain sees it as convex, even re-interpreting the lighting as coming from an unnatural direction to make this possible. Only when the mask is seen side on (middle) can we step aside from our hard-wired prejudice and perceive the shape as it is in reality.

Similar prejudices distort our appreciation of probability. If a tossed coin comes down heads twenty times in a row we are surprised – and may even conclude that some

supernatural force or trickery is at work. But if it comes down H (heads) T (tails) then T H H T H T T T H H H H T T T H T T we are not surprised at all – even though the chances of both sequences are identical.

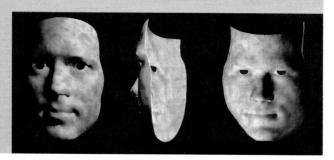

SENSORY CROSSOVER

Usually, the brain responds to visual information by constructing visual images, while vibrations in a certain range are experienced as sound. But this basic interpretation of reality is not common to everyone. Some people have a condition known as synaesthesia, in which visual information is also experienced as sound, and vibrations as images. Other senses may be 'mixed' in this way. One woman 'tasted' words; the name 'Richard', for example, gave her an intense sensation of chocolate.

Many writers, artists and musicians, including Nabokov, Messiaen and Hockney, have reported experiences of synaesthesia, and the Russian painter Wassily Kandinsky made use of it in his work. 'Colour', he said, 'is the keyboard, the eyes are the hammers, the soul is the piano with many strings.'

Sally and Ann. At the beginning, Sally is given a sweet, which she places in a box before leaving the room. While she is away, Ann takes the sweet out of the box and places it in a different box. Sally then returns, and the children are asked: 'Which box will Sally think the sweet is in?'

Children under the age of about four usually answer that Sally thinks the sweet is in the second box, because they assume that the doll shares their own view of the world, and are unable to understand that Sally lacks information that they have. Over this age, however, children realise that Sally's view is different – that she did not see the sweet being switched, so she will expect it to be in the box she left it in. The inbuilt theory of mind that allows them to work out another person's perspective is working.

FACT: Perception is altered by mood. Depressed people, for example, see life quite literally as more grey than people in a buoyant state of mind, because the colour areas of their brains are less active.

Mirroring emotions

The theory of mind has its physical basis in brain cells known as mirror neurons. When activated, these cells produce a wide range of perceptions, emotions and compulsions to act – just like other brain cells. But what is special about them is the way they are activated. Unlike most other neurons, which respond to a wide range of stimuli, mirror cells become active only when the response they produce in the person is first observed in another. So, for example, when one individual sees another making an expression of disgust, the 'disgust' mirror neurons become active, producing a similar feeling. Mirror neurons give us built-in empathy – an automatic, intuitive sense of what another person is experiencing.

R.D. LAING – UNDERSTANDING SCHIZOPHRENIA

The Scottish psychiatrist Ronald David Laing (1927–1989) was one of the most influential and controversial thinkers of the 1960s. He questioned orthodoxy, arguing that the perceptions of people considered to be mentally ill are as valid in their own terms as those of 'normal' individuals. Laing pointed out that almost any behaviour could be taken as a symptom of schizophrenia, allowing psychiatrists to give a medical label to those who simply refused to conform to the expectations of family and society. For Laing, schizophrenia was a way of experiencing the world, not a disease; mental 'illness' could in fact be an existential journey – a cure for misery rooted in childhood and family.

Born in Glasgow in 1927, Laing's own family upbringing was turbulent. After completing his medical training in 1958, he worked in a British Army psychiatric unit. His book *Sanity, Madness and the Family* (1964), which argued that schizophrenia could be caused by communication breakdown within the family, established Laing's international reputation, and he continued high-profile clinical work into the 1970s. Later, Laing's intellectual standing was compromised by his fascination with mysticism and he eventually lost his licence to practise medicine in Britain.

John Nash was a brilliant mathematician, who was awarded the Nobel Prize for Economics in 1994. For many years he was afflicted by schizophrenic delusions, in which he believed that aliens were passing him information.

In 1959, a colleague visiting him asked how, as 'a man devoted to reason and logical proof', he could believe that extraterrestrials were recruiting him to save the world. Nash replied that 'the ideas I had about supernatural beings came to me the same way that my mathematical ideas did. So I took them seriously'.

Contact through conversation

Another, more obvious, way of finding out how another person is perceiving things is by talking. Telling each other about our experiences is important because it allows us to reconcile opposing views. Say, for example, a couple go out to buy a sofa for their home. He wants black leather, she wants red velvet. They could simply state their desires, disagree, and feel mystified at the apparent error of the other's way of thinking. But if he explains that he thinks the black leather is elegant and modern, and she explains that, to her, red velvet is warm and comfortable, they can at least try out the other's point of view and perhaps see its merits.

Most everyday differences in perception that cloud our dealings with other people can be resolved through discussion and compromise. However, some are so fundamental that it is impossible to bridge the chasm between two different perceptions. Sometimes, a person's view of the world is so bizarre that it cannot be shared by others. People with such extreme perceptions are generally regarded as psychotic – dislocated from reality.

Delusions and psychosis

The most extreme psychotic perceptions are held by people who suffer from schizophrenia. To schizophrenics, their perceptions seem to come from the real world, but they are actually made up largely of hallucinations (see page 57). The sufferer cannot detect that the hallucinations are internally generated, but instead seeks a plausible explanation for their origin – perhaps that voices have been beamed into his or her mind by malevolent aliens.

Schizophrenic delusions are warped perceptions that can sometimes lead to disaster. But there are many other, more subtle, ways in which non-consensual viewpoints can wreak havoc in society. The distorted world-views of despots like Hitler, egomaniacs like Idi Amin, and cult leaders like Charles Manson are far more threatening than the delusions of schizophrenics because they are combined with a persuasiveness that seduces others into sharing their pathological assumptions. The terrible outcome of such distortions of social values underscores the importance of holding on to one's own sense of reality – and constantly testing beliefs against the widest range of evidence, rather than relying on the opinions of selected others to confirm or deny them.

> **"If I don't know I don't know, I think I know. If I don't know I know, I think I don't know."**
>
> R.D. Laing, psychiatrist

The doors of perception

Mind-altering drugs have featured in the work of many writers, poets and artists — either as subject matter, or as the means by which they achieved their creative insights.

Psychotropic drugs have influenced the work of countless writers. In a tradition that goes back hundreds of years, many prominent writers have related experiences of drug-induced altered states or have used these states to inspire their work.

The 'stately pleasure dome' in Xanadu, described in Samuel Taylor Coleridge's epic poem *Kubla Khan* (1816), is largely the product of the poet's opium-inspired fantasies. And the near-transcendental appreciation of the natural world and the Gothic fantasies of poets such as Scott, Shelley, Wordsworth, Byron and Poe owe much to the mind-altering effects of drugs. One of the earliest first-person accounts of drug experiences, and the effect of drugs on society, is Thomas de Quincey's *Confessions of an Opium Eater*. Published in 1821, de Quincey's book describes his own and others' attempts to find peace and transcendence in the 'gathering agitation' of the Industrial Revolution, and his discovery that 'some merely physical agencies can and do assist the faculty of dreaming and ... beyond all others is opium'.

Expanding horizons

In the late 19th and early 20th century there were few legal restrictions on drugs: opium, cannabis and, latterly, cocaine were more or less freely available to those who could afford them. Writers of the period were quick to experiment with their possible benefits. In France, Victor Hugo, Alexandre Dumas and Charles Baudelaire, together with other artists and writers, formed 'Le Club de Hachichines' specifically to extol the virtues of cannabis as an aid to creativity.

Many of the strange sequences in Lewis Carroll's *Alice Through the Looking-Glass* (1872) are perfect descriptions of the effects of 'magic' mushrooms, and rumour has it that *The Strange Case of Dr Jekyll and Mr Hyde* (1886), completed by Robert Louis Stevenson in six days and six nights, was written while the author was high on cocaine.

Prohibition and rebellion

In the 20th century, attitudes towards drug use began to change. A spate of books railed about the dangers of drugs — Aldous Huxley's *Brave New World* (1932), for example, characterised the fictional 'soma' as the route to moral degeneracy — and 'dope scandals' in Hollywood revealed that many of the clean-cut heroes of the silver screen were drug addicts. The shock ushered in a new age of prohibition, and the start of the 'war against drugs' that still rages today.

It was not until the 1950s that drugs again started to be used openly by writers as a means of inspiration. Interestingly, it was Huxley himself who helped to reverse the climate with his celebrated

Literary addict Sir Arthur Conan Doyle's detective hero, Sherlock Holmes, was addicted to both laudanum and cocaine. While conceding the damaging physical effects of cocaine, Holmes remarks: 'I find it so transcendentally stimulating and clarifying to the Mind that its secondary action is of small moment.'

investigation of psychedelic drugs. Huxley wrote an essay, titled *The Doors of Perception,* after experimenting with hallucinogens, including mescaline and LSD. Of his first mescaline experience he wrote: 'It was without doubt the most extraordinary and significant experience this side of Beatific vision.' And he described looking at a flower during a drug trip as seeing 'what Adam had seen on the morning of creation – the miracle, moment by moment, of naked existence ... words like "grace" and "transfiguration" came to mind'.

This work established Huxley as a propagandist for hallucinogenic drugs, and its publication brought them to wide public attention. It created a storm in literary circles, with some critics hailing it as a major intellectual breakthrough and others as incoherent nonsense. Today it is widely regarded as a classic.

Aldous Huxley

The use of hallucinogens as an expression of rebellion characterised the 'beat generation' of the 1950s, setting the scene for an explosion of drug-related writing in the 1960s. This included the proselytising works of Harvard psychologist Timothy Leary, whose stated ambition was to 'turn on the world'. But Leary went too far for the authorities – he, along with several others of his generation, were hounded by police and finally arrested and imprisoned.

Since then, drugs have continued to feature almost routinely in contemporary fiction and film, though the largely uncritical attitude towards them has given way to a more wary appreciation of their benefits and risks.

> **"What came through that closed door was the realisation ... of Love as the primary and fundamental cosmic fact."**
>
> Aldous Huxley, from *The Doors of Perception*

DRUGS AND THE BEAT GENERATION

The conformity of 1950s America gave birth to a generation of bohemian writers – the 'beats'. The group, which included Jack Kerouac, Allan Ginsberg and William S. Burroughs, created a new vision of art that expressed a bitter disaffection with materialistic post-war society. They teamed drugs like benzedrine, LSD, peyote, morphine, opium and cocaine with Eastern mysticism and elements of Western avant-garde, such as dadaism and jazz, in their search for 'the ancient heavenly connection'. Their work – once derided by the establishment – is now considered to be highly influential, although it was produced at great cost to the authors. Kerouac died a severely depressed alcoholic at the age of 47, while Burroughs spent many years battling his addiction to heroin.

Beat movie A scene from the 1992 film of William Burroughs' 1959 novel, *The Naked Lunch.* The vivid portrayal of drug addiction drew upon the author's own experience.

3 THE UNCONSCIOUS BRAIN

By definition, our unconscious minds are unknown to us: if we could ponder our unconscious mental processes, they would no longer be unconscious. Although we have all experienced the forces that our unconscious can exert on our conscious thinking and behaviour, discovering the exact way in which our minds work beneath our consciousness is not a straightforward matter.

Sigmund Freud famously believed he had discovered what was in the unconscious mind – a dark, seething mass of repressed sexual desires. Other thinkers built on Freud's theories, bringing mysticism and surrealist ideas to bear on the issue. Today, psychologists take perhaps the saner view that, in general, the unconscious is involved in much the same things as the conscious mind. The surprising element is that, in some ways, the unconscious can outsmart the conscious brain. This modern view has given us new routes towards an understanding of the unconscious, and answers are emerging to such questions as: how do our brains work so effectively on autopilot? How powerful is subliminal perception? And is unconscious learning really a possibility?

WHAT IS THE UNCONSCIOUS?

Until a little over a century ago, few people believed in the unconscious: the contents of the mind were, by definition, conscious. But today's psychologists agree with Freud that our lives are ruled by thoughts and feelings of which we are unaware.

When we sink into deep sleep, faint, or have a general anaesthetic, we are unconscious. Being in this state is impossible to describe because it isn't like anything – we are simply unaware of feeling or thinking. It isn't surprising, therefore, that the very idea of an active unconscious was scorned by self-respecting thinkers, from the ancient Greeks onwards. An ancient Greek who had attempted to discuss the unconscious would have been laughed out of the symposium. The contents of your mind were by definition conscious: if you wanted to know what was going on inside your head, all you had to do was look inside with your 'inner eye'.

Even by the 18th century, philosophers such as David Hume and John Locke regarded all mental events – thinking, knowing and feeling – as taking place on the playing field of awareness. As Locke wrote: 'to imprint anything on the mind, without the mind's perceiving it, seems to me hardly intelligible'. Minds were transparent – although you could only know for certain what was going on inside your own.

Towards the unconscious

So what brought us to a belief in the unconscious, and the acknowledgment that our lives are ruled by motivations of which we are unaware? The first steps were taken by the Austrian physician, Franz Anton Mesmer. Experimenting with hypnotism in Paris at the end of the 18th century, Mesmer showed that unconscious thoughts could exert an effect on the body, producing paralysis or insensibility to pain. His work was taken up by French neurologist Jean Martin Charcot, who used hypnosis to induce and study hysteria – a medical condition often involving a mixture of psychological and physical symptoms such as blindness, paralysis and amnesia. Charcot was assisted in these studies by Sigmund Freud, then a brilliant medical student. Together with his mentor, Freud elaborated the theory that the symptoms of hysteria were a disguised means of keeping emotionally charged memories under mental lock and key in the unconscious mind. This led to his development of the technique of psychoanalysis to gain access to the unconscious and effect 'cures'. Freud's theory that unconscious thoughts were responsible for much of human behaviour caused an outrage. Apart from the appalling

> "Man cannot persist long in a conscious state; he must throw himself back into the Unconscious, for his roots live there."
>
> Goethe, writer and philosopher (1749–1832)

Austrian physician Franz Anton Mesmer (1734–1815) took Paris by storm in the 1780s with his demonstrations of 'magnetic influence'. Mesmer (far left) believed that he could cure diseases using his hands to channel 'animal magnetism', a force he thought related to physical magnetism. Mesmer often gave dramatic public performances of this strange art. The magnetic theory proved to be false — Mesmer in fact was hypnotising his patients by looking, talking and touching.

notion that respectable members of society were all being driven by unthinkable sexual desires, where did that leave notions of free will and responsibility? Nevertheless, Freud's ideas became increasingly accepted and remain highly influential. As post-Freudians, we are all happy to talk about unconscious motives, and ideas like repression and denial have entered the popular vocabulary. In a way, Freud's work has made psychologists of us all.

Modern times

Since Freud's time, scientists have moved away from Freud's model of the unconscious — a potent broth of traumatic memories and repression that only the psychoanalyst could clarify. Today, the more that scientists study the unconscious, the more remarkable it seems. Over the last 40 years, experimental psychologists have found that people constantly engage in all sorts of mental activity that is not simply repressed but is totally beyond the scope of consciousness. All sorts of highly sophisticated mental activities — searching memory, solving problems, making inferences — are carried out at an unconscious level. As the capabilities of the unconscious mind become ever more evident, some researchers have even begun to wonder whether we need consciousness at all.

FACT FILE

WORDS TO DESCRIBE THE UNCONSCIOUS

Different words are used to refer to mental experiences outside consciousness.

• 'Preconscious' and 'subliminal' refer to experiences just below the threshold of consciousness.
• 'Unconscious' and 'subconscious' often indicate a more profound inaccessibility.
• Psychologists also refer to 'implicit' (in contrast with 'explicit') knowledge — that is, knowledge we have without being able to state it.

THE ROBOT WITHIN

When today's psychologists talk about the unconscious, they don't mean the independent force that Freud imagined. Rather, the unconscious is seen more as a network of automatons, each of which controls an aspect of behaviour.

FACT: Olympic sprinters leave the starting block one-tenth of a second after the pistol has fired. They don't hear it consciously because it takes about twice as long to become conscious of sensory stimuli.

Imagine that you are walking through a wood that you know to be full of venomous snakes. Suddenly you jump backwards. As you are in the air, you become dimly aware of something long, thin and brown that was in your path; you have just avoided treading on a snake. Yet when you started your jump, you weren't aware of anything dangerous at all.

This is an example of an unconscious response initiated not by the cortex – the thinking, judging part of the brain – but by an autonomous processing unit, a subsystem that produces automatic reactions. Your ears detect a signal of danger (the rustling of the snake in the grass), and a signal is sent via the brain's auditory system directly to the amygdala, a structure that controls fear response. Because it bypasses the cortex, the 'danger' signal causes you to move that much faster, gaining you vital milliseconds that may save your life.

Unconscious helpers

Countless other subsystems exist in the brain. Moment by moment, this army of unconscious helpers

Automatic skills It takes time and a lot of practice to master complex skills such as touch-typing, but they eventually become automated processes controlled by the unconscious brain.

handles all sorts of complicated processing of which we are not aware. They control blood pressure, build our three-dimensional images of the world from the two-dimensional information coming from the retina, and effortlessly produce grammatical sentences. When we learn a new physical skill – like typing or playing the piano – we are actually training subsystems to carry out sets of complex functions automatically. And even tasks that many people imagine depend on awareness – such as an understanding of speech – are in fact carried out by these unconscious helpers. Each one of the separate processing units is, in the words of one researcher, a 'mindless simpleton' because it can do only one thing – but it does that thing very well and reports its actions back to the central executive of consciousness. So rather than consciousness being seen as the boss, controlling the mind like a general, it looks increasingly like the figurehead of a large organisation – or perhaps a government minister who is backed up by an army of invisible civil servants.

THINK AGAIN! SPACE GAMES AND REFLEX SKILLS

Experiments carried out on board the space shuttle *Columbia* in 1998 demonstrate how hard it is to override unconscious processing with conscious thought. Astronauts on the shuttle threw balls to one another and attempted to catch them – a straightforward task back on Earth, but not so easy in low-gravity conditions where balls move far more slowly. Even though the astronauts could clearly see the balls drifting toward them, their hands moved far faster than they needed to in anticipation of a ball's trajectory – they were in the right place long before the ball reached them.

The explanation for this is that ball-catching is under the control of unconscious modules in the brain, and these modules have been 'programmed' under conditions of normal gravity. Used inappropriately in the low-gravity environment on board

the shuttle, they cause errors in the judgement of motion.

The experiments also tell us something surprising about the abilities of top cricket and tennis players. The popular view is that good ball players have extra-fast reflexes that enable them to get the bat or racquet to a ball moving at well over 100mph. In fact, their reflexes are often average; what distinguishes a skilled sportsperson is the ability to delay the unconscious response for a fraction of a second. With more time for unconscious processing, the 'intuitive' reaction becomes that much more accurate.

Lunch on the go Astronaut Michael Baker chases a sandwich on the flight deck of shuttle *Atlantis*.

The Goodale illusion Psychologist Mel Goodale has used this illusion to demonstrate how the unconscious brain can make better judgements than the conscious mind. Look at the circles in the centre of the two patterns below and try to judge whether the central circle in the left-hand pattern is bigger, smaller, or the same size as the one in the right-hand pattern.

Blind vision

An astonishing demonstration of the abilities of our unconscious pathways comes from studies of a bizarre condition known as blindsight. Graham, a typical sufferer, is totally blind on the right side of his visual field as a result of an accident. Experimenters asked Graham what he could see on the right side; predictably, his reply was 'nothing'. Then the experimenters set up a projector screen in Graham's blind patch. Onto it they projected spots of light, shapes and words and asked Graham to guess what was out there. Remarkably, he could 'guess' with great accuracy. In fact, Graham could see, but he was not conscious of seeing because his vision was being processed by the unconscious helpers alone.

Equally amazing is the fact that the unconscious brain is often better than the conscious mind at interpreting data from our senses. The conscious mind is quite easily fooled by illusion: for example, flat paintings that use perspective often appear to have real depth. But the unconscious is much less likely to be taken in – perhaps because it is designed for fast evaluation and action. The Goodale illusion is a good example. This consists of two circular wooden counters, identical in size and shape, one surrounded by a cluster of smaller counters, the other by bigger ones. The conscious brain cannot help but see an illusion – the counter surrounded by the smaller chips always looks the bigger. But the unconscious robot pathway 'sees' them as identical: if someone is asked to pick up the central counters, careful measurement of the space between their fingers at the moment of contact reveals an identical gap.

Real lives *THE ARTISTIC UNCONSCIOUS*

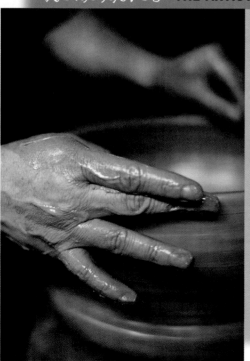

Artist Anthony deliberately 'switches off' his conscious mind when he works to allow his unconscious to take over.

'Several hours of my working week are spent drawing figures from life. There are good days, when every mark on the paper goes just where it should, and bad days when the simplest drawing seems laboured and clumsy. I put this down to being in or out of "the flow". One way I've found to help get into flow is to do the drawing blind – that is, to look at the model while I work, instead of looking at what my hand is doing. When I do this, I usually find the drawing improves.

'Also, when I'm throwing a production run of pots, I need to start with clay pieces of a consistent size. I roll out a long cylinder of clay, then twist off a chunk for each bowl, weigh it, and add or subtract more until it is exactly right. Again, there are good days when I estimate the amount correctly each time, and bad days. Recently I tried turning my head away just at the moment I came to twist off the clay. The result was an immediate improvement. The pieces were within a gram or so of the target weight every time – accurate enough to go right ahead and use it without any adjustments.

'I've come to believe that this sort of instinctive perception plays a crucial role in areas that are often attributed to some mysterious "talent". In fact, artistic talent may just be an ability to let my unconscious get on with the job.'

A new role for consciousness?

Another set of experiments, conducted in the 1960s by the Californian physiologist Benjamin Libet, underlines the extraordinary abilities of the unconscious and challenges our cherished notion of free will.

Libet connected subjects to EEG monitors that recorded their brain waves, in particular one type of electrical pulse known as a 'readiness potential', which signals that the brain is preparing to make a consciously willed movement. The subjects were asked to watch a dot move clockwise on a screen. Libet would then ask them to lift a finger whenever they felt the urge and to note where the dot was at that moment. Remarkably, the EEG readings showed that the readiness potential appeared about half a second before subjects said that they had 'decided' to move. In other words, some combination of the unconscious modules was preparing for a move before the subjects had consciously decided to move.

If the unconscious can do all these things – if it can see, hear and take decisions before we are even aware of them, if it can process language and trigger emotional responses – then what exactly is the role, and indeed the point, of consciousness? In fact, the unconscious and conscious parts of our minds need one another and work in close partnership.

Consciousness – the executive

Brain scans reveal quite different patterns of mental activity when we think consciously about a task (for example, the first time we try to play the piano) and when our unconscious 'simpletons' handle a task unaided (when we can play the piano fluently). When we think consciously, big areas of the brain 'light up' on the scans, as we mobilise our mental resources to deal with an unfamiliar situation. Unconscious activity, in contrast, produces a much fainter trace on a brain scan. So consciousness takes charge of novelty, while commonplace processing takes place unconsciously.

Consciousness also has a crucial 'executive' function in the mind: we have only one body and so consciousness must decide between conflicting unconscious instructions about where to move the legs or turn the head, for example. Consciousness has power of veto over the unconscious – free won't rather than free will – so we are not just slaves to the robot within.

FOCUS ON *UNCONSCIOUS ACCURACY*

Consciousness personalises our world. Our conscious perceptions are determined by our beliefs, interests, fears and preoccupations, as well as by what is 'out there'. In contrast, the kind of unconscious processing that we use to make physical (rather than verbal) judgments are less subject to these idiosyncratic influences, and consequently these judgments are often the more reliable.

This effect becomes obvious when people are asked, for example, to estimate the steepness of a hill. Asked for a verbal judgment, almost everyone overestimates the gradient, although younger and fitter people will think the slope is less steep than older or unfit people. But when people are asked simply to tilt their hand to match the slope of the hill, they do so with considerably greater accuracy.

UNCONSCIOUS THINKING

Everything we think and say is informed by unconscious processing. Our emotional reactions, beliefs, opinions – even our most carefully deliberated decisions – are determined to a large extent by mental processes outside our conscious awareness.

FACT: In court cases, 'good-looking' people are assumed to be innocent more often than average.

Conscious perceptions are a bit like takeaway meals. By the time we get them they have been processed, packaged, transported and presented for consumption by a chain of invisible workers. Their original ingredients may no longer even be recognisable.

The 'workers' that produce the contents of consciousness are specialised brain modules that process raw information arriving at our sense organs into sights, sounds, feelings, thoughts, decisions and beliefs. Only some of this processing reaches consciousness, with the vast majority remaining unconscious. This unconscious processing is vitally important, constantly directing our actions by moulding our conscious decisions, or, sometimes, by overriding them.

The chemical unconscious

Consider, for example, what happens when you notice someone looking at you in a restaurant or when queuing for a bus. As soon as you make eye contact, the amount of the neurotransmitter dopamine (sometimes called the brain's pleasure chemical) in your brain is affected. Typically dopamine levels rise if the stranger's face is attractive (symmetrical, young and smiling) and fall if it is unattractive (asymmetrical, aged and frowning). Significantly, this reaction occurs before you have

Real lives

A LIFE IN FREEZE FRAME

Unconscious processing units in the brain control many very specific aspects of everyday actions. When they go wrong, the results can be quite strange.

June can see perfectly well. She can perceive colour and shape, and she has no trouble recognising objects. But a crucial element of her visual world is missing – she has no sense of movement. Everyday scenes appear as if illuminated by strobe lighting – as a sequence of still frames with the intervening bits blotted out. June has difficulty in pouring tea or coffee into a cup because the fluid does not seem to flow, but appears to be frozen. What's more, she cannot stop pouring at the correct time because she can't see the liquid moving up in the cup. She also finds it hard to follow a conversation because she cannot see other people's faces moving. And being in a room with people walking around is unsettling: they seem to appear suddenly in different places. June cannot cross a street because she is unable to judge the speed of approaching cars: 'When I'm looking at the car first, it seems far away', says June. 'But then, when I want to cross the road, suddenly the car is very near.' June has learned to 'estimate' the distance of moving vehicles from their sound, but her world remains a bizarrely disjointed place.

consciously registered the face, so by the time the image does arrive in consciousness, your unconscious mind has already 'approved' or 'disapproved' of the face. With no way of knowing what is happening to your dopamine levels, you naturally suppose that your first assessment of the person is based on rational deliberation.

It is not hard to see how such unconscious processing feeds into behaviour. For example, candidates for jobs are likely to fare better at interview if they are attractive rather than unattractive; interviewers do not consciously judge by looks, they just know that one candidate makes them feel hopeful and the other disappointed.

Patterns of influence

Every idea, attitude and emotion that we hold in mind is encoded in the patterns of neural firing in our brains. Some of these ideas can be dragged out into consciousness, where they can be moulded and modified by reflection, thought and experience. But others – like the dopamine effect described above – are permanently hidden in the back rooms of the brain and only manifest themselves by their effect on behaviour.

When these patterns are inactive they are 'out of mind' and do not influence our actions. But many patterns fire away at a low rate – not enough to become part of consciousness, but enough to feed into the unconscious information processing that precedes consciousness. These habitual thought processes form a background template of ideas, beliefs and prejudices through which all new information is filtered.

These background, unconscious thought patterns include many of the fixed ideas that we have about the physical world. A good example is the idea of 'object permanence'. We all know that objects do not cease to exist simply because they are hidden from view. This assumption develops in all human infants at the age of about eight months – long before they have enough experience to have arrived at it by deduction. Similarly, we all tend to assign intentions to moving inanimate objects: an observer who sees a small ball rolling along followed by a larger ball will invariably

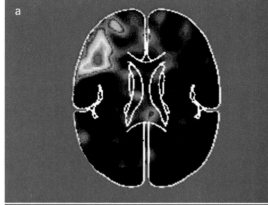

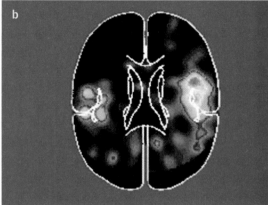

Practice and the brain Different brain areas are used when we are new to a task and need consciously to focus on it, compared to when we are practised at it when less conscious areas take over. Here, a verbal task requiring rapid, conscious thought (a) shows high activity in the left prefrontal cortex. After some practice (b), a less 'conscious' area in the right cortex becomes more active during the task.

THINK AGAIN!   PROCESSING MEANING

It's tempting to think that the unconscious modules that process information lack the sophistication of the conscious mind. But studies suggest it is the conscious mind that sometimes makes the clumsier distinctions.

In one experiment, people were shown a sentence with a word missing. It read: 'She looked very (blank) in her new coat'. The subjects wore headphones through which experimenters could relay spoken words. Half of the subjects were played the word 'snug' at normal volume; half were played the same word subliminally – that is, so quietly that subjects were not conscious of hearing it. The subjects were then asked to 'fill in' the gap, choosing between the words 'smug' and 'cosy'.

The experimenters found that those who could clearly hear the word 'snug' were more likely to choose 'smug', but those who could hear it only subliminally preferred 'cosy'. This means that the conscious mind was being directed more by the sound of the word, while the unconscious concentrated on meaning – an aspect that seems more sophisticated and more useful than mere sound.

interpret the scene as the large ball 'chasing' the smaller one. And the larger the object, the more 'intentional' it will be perceived to be.

These deep-rooted ideas probably evolved because they were of great survival value to our ancestors: any animal that assumes an object is still present when it is hidden is exercising caution – and is less likely to be eaten by a predator that hides behind a bush. Similarly, it is safer to assume that moving objects have motives – a fast-approaching blur may be a wind-blown branch, but it may also be a vicious animal.

But these quick and easy evaluations are not always useful in a sophisticated environment. The 'folk physics' wired into the brain makes it easy for magicians to fool people, and means that we find it difficult to grasp scientific concepts that conflict with our intuitions. And rules of thumb that were once useful when we lived in small tribes and depended on physical strength for survival are now potentially damaging. For example, the idea that people whom we resemble physically are more likely to be friendly now forms the basis of social pathologies, such as racism and elitist prejudices.

Learning from experience

Many of the things we learn are held in our minds unconsciously. People can be 'primed' to react to something in a particular way by exposing them to an influential stimulus for such a short time that they do not register it consciously – that is, it is presented subliminally. In one laboratory experiment, researchers divided volunteers into two groups. An image was then flashed up in front of the volunteers so quickly – for about 150 milliseconds – that they were not even aware of seeing it. One group was shown an image of a leaf and the other an image of a cup. The two groups were then shown the word 'tea' and asked to add a second word. Most of the group that had been exposed to the image of the leaf wrote 'tea leaf', while most of those who had been shown the cup wrote 'tea cup'. Yet when asked, none of the volunteers were aware that their choice of words had been influenced by a visual image.

Many of our behavioural tendencies are primed by past experience. If a child is bitten by a dog, for example, she is likely to think 'danger' whenever she sees a dog later in life, even if the original incident is long-forgotten and buried in the unconscious. She is also likely to rationalise her fear of dogs – explaining to herself that 'all dogs are vicious and unpredictable' – because her brain seeks an explanation for her irrational fear. Such 'post-rationalisation' of behaviour has been demonstrated by many psychologists. In one experiment, researchers invited women to choose between two pairs of stockings, which, unknown to the subjects, were identical. Nearly all the subjects chose the pair which was presented to their right. This was predictable, because previous studies had already shown that people favour that side in all sorts of ways. But when asked why they had picked that product, the subjects did not mention its placement. Instead they claimed to have detected some superiority of quality such as feel, texture, or colour … imaginary differences that gave spurious reason to what was an entirely unconscious choice.

Another vital unconscious influence on our behaviour is known as implicit learning. We can learn to do something – even something complex, such as playing the piano to an expert level – without consciously knowing or being able to say what we have learned. This also applies to non-physical skills: when we use language – speaking, listening or reading – much of the mental work is in fact carried out at an unconscious level. You can see this when you find yourself unable to describe the complex grammatical reasons behind your choice of a word (such as 'I' or 'me') in conversation, even though your unconscious mind has correctly selected this word in a fraction of a second.

In a laboratory experiment, UK psychologists Diane Berry and Donald Broadbent used a complex 'control task' to study implicit learning. In the task, a simulated factory had to be 'managed' to produce a specific level of output. Some people were given explicit information on the output-related variables, while others were simply left to learn through practice. Remarkably, the explicit information was found not to improve performance at all. At the end of the experiment, those in either group who had learned successfully to control the output were all unable to explain how they did it. This finding has clear consequences for how best to encourage learning: it seems that, even in areas that are more to do with judgment and decision-making, book-learned knowledge is no substitute for hands-on experience.

Unconscious skills
Even when the conscious mind is fully engaged, such as when making decisions, we are in fact constantly tapping into 'implicit' knowledge that we have acquired without being able to express it.

SUGGESTIBILITY

Sometimes we think we have made up our own minds, when in fact they have been made up for us. None of us is immune to the influence of strong ideas forced upon us by other people, and much of our behaviour owes less to free will than it does to the will of others.

Humans are social animals. Many of our higher conscious functions – our ideals, beliefs, standards and even personalities – are products not only of our private experience and genetic make-up but of the influence of other people. Usually these influences are positive: in childhood, our beliefs are shaped by our family members and teachers, and later in life other people present us with new ideas that we can adopt or reject as we choose. But sometimes other people's ideas impinge on our conscious – or on our unconscious – minds with considerable persuasive effect. They change our attitudes and behaviour without our overt consent, as if we have surrendered up part of our consciousness.

Social pressure

Experiments in the 1950s by psychologist Solomon Asch demonstrates how suggestions teamed with social pressure can overwhelm our own thinking. Asch presented groups of eight subjects with a card showing three lines of different length. He then asked the subjects to point out which line on the card best matched the length of a reference line on another card. The answer was obvious, but apart from one person in each group, all the group members were 'plants', briefed to give an incorrect answer. Startlingly, in 75 per cent of the experiments, the one 'innocent' member of the group went along with the others, denying the evidence from his or her own senses.

> **"Half the money spent on advertising is wasted. The problem is in finding out which half."**
>
> Lord Leverhulme, industrialist

We are all suggestible in the sense that we yield, to some extent, to social norms. But human suggestibility is also open to deliberate abuse by people who want to persuade or control others – to change not only their behaviour but their

The power of advertising

Over the last century, there has been a gradual change in the persuasive tactics used to market a product. Earlier advertisements tended to be straightforwardly informative, describing the superior features of a product. Today's advertisements are often more suggestive, creating a desire for products by associating them with glamour and sexual appeal.

FOCUS ON COERCIVE PERSUASION

Coercive persuasion techniques are well understood by psychologists, and depend on some or all of the following key factors:

1. Physical and emotional stress, especially deprivation of food, sleep and exercise. Social isolation (creating loneliness) is alternated with group sessions that introduce the new beliefs.

2. Simplistic explanations of 'personal problems', together with simplistic 'answers', for example: 'Your parents are giving you a hard time, so reject them completely and join our group.'

3. A leader who appears to offer love, care, acceptance and answers. Cults are typically run by charismatic leaders who demand loyalty and adoration.

4. Influence of other group members, providing praise, emotional support and other reinforcement. Pyramid selling schemes often involve 'introducers' who encourage individuals to join, and talk up their money-making prospects.

5. Some form of entrapment. Often this starts with small things, such as attending a meeting or donating some money. Later these may become more demanding, perhaps involving 'buying in' to a sales organisation or living permanently with a group.

6. Control of information and activities. For example, once a person has become a committed member of a cult, the group will typically dictate what is allowed and whom can be contacted.

underlying beliefs and feelings too. In its most extreme form, the abuse of human suggestibility is called 'brainwashing'. The term was first coined in the 1950s during the Korean War, when Chinese Communists subjected American prisoners of war to various forms of mental and physical torture in an attempt to change their political attitudes. The Koreans 'converted' 7000 POWs to take part in pro-communist broadcasts and other forms of collaboration. Their techniques included food and sleep deprivation, isolation, highly organised group activities, repetitive chanting and forced 'confessions'.

Gentler persuasion?

While brainwashing relies on the use of torture, imprisonment, repetitive music and even drugs, there are less physically aggressive forms of coercion that can be almost as powerful. The use of such techniques – known as 'coercive persuasion' – has been brought to prominence by cults, religious sects and pressure sales organisations over the last 40 years.

The coercive persuasion process typically occurs in steps over a period of weeks or months. Suggestibility expert Philip Zimbardo has found that, while some people are more susceptible to coercive tactics than others, we are all liable to be influenced by such techniques. Those who have succumbed can recover with the help of cognitive-behavioural therapists that can reverse the process. Ironically, the treatment may involve techniques similar to those used in the first place.

In a milder form, coercion is also the basis of everyday advertising. The central aim of advertising is to make you want something that you do not already have. Perhaps the most common technique is the association of the item with pleasant feelings – what psychologists call Pavlovian conditioning. For example, a car will be shown with attractive people in beautiful surroundings, accompanied by evocative music. Your previous satisfaction with your present vehicle and lifestyle may be replaced with a vague hankering for a sleeker new model.

Cult persuasion The 'Children of God' cult is believed to have used coercive persuasion techniques to recruit new members, targeting vulnerable young people and encouraging them to cut off contact with their families. Here, members of the cult sing together before a meal.

UNCONSCIOUS PROBLEM SOLVING

One of the most fascinating aspects of the unconscious mind is the way in which it can solve problems while the conscious mind is occupied with other matters. Many examples of unconscious problem solving come from everyday situations, but there are also well-documented cases where these processes have led to important scientific breakthroughs and artistic inspiration.

We are all familiar with the 'tip of the tongue' phenomenon. We can't remember a name despite thinking hard about it, but the name suddenly springs to mind later on when we are doing something else. Many of us also solve problems when we dream. Consider the following example: Clive moved house, but after unpacking couldn't find his watch anywhere. He kept looking, but without success. One night, he tried an experiment: he visualised the watch in all its detail before falling asleep. That night he had a dream in which he was wearing an old jacket. The next morning he went to his wardrobe and checked the jacket's pockets. Sure enough, the watch was there. His conscious efforts at remembering where the watch was had been fruitless, but his unconscious mind solved the problem for him.

Ring of dreams

Several famous scientists and inventors have solved problems through their dreams. Perhaps the best known case was German chemist Friedrich Kekulé, who attempted to elucidate the chemical structure of the benzene in the 1860s. Kekulé knew that benzene was an organic compound – that is, one made up of linked carbon atoms; he also knew its formula, but its structure – the way the atoms were linked together – remained an enigma. This is Kekulé's story, in his own words:

'I was sitting writing in my textbook, but the work did not progress; my thoughts were elsewhere. I turned my chair to the fire and dozed … the atoms were gambolling before my eyes … My mental eye, rendered more acute by repeated visions of the kind, could now distinguish larger structures of manifold conformation: long rows sometimes more closely fitted together all twining and twisting in snake-like motion. But look! What was that? One of the snakes had seized hold of its own tail, and the form whirled mockingly before my eyes. As if by a flash of lightning I awoke; and this time also I spent the rest of the night in working out the consequences of the hypothesis.'

FACT FILE

FAMOUS DREAMERS

It is not only scientists and inventors who have benefited from unconscious problem solving; many artists and musicians have been inspired by dreams too.

• Mendeleyev saw a complete layout of the chemicals in the Periodic Table in a dream.

• Herschel dreamed about the planet now known as Uranus in a dream, before he discovered it.

• Edison, an inventor with more than 1000 patents to his name, sometimes slept at his workbench holding weights in his hands: when the weights fell, they would wake him and he would recall his dreams – often leading to new inventions.

• Salvador Dali produced many of his images from dreams. He used to deliberately deprive himself of sleep in order to induce dream-like states and visions that drew upon his unconscious mind.

• Beethoven, Wagner and Stravinsky all heard music – ranging from fragments to entire canons – in their dreams.

• Bob Dylan wrote songs based on what he heard in his dreams.

Inspired by his dream, Kekulé wondered whether the benzene molecule was ring-shaped – like the snake holding its own tail. When he tested out his idea, he found that it fitted all the known facts about benzene and its chemical nature; his discovery was an enormous step in the development of organic chemistry.

Medical inspiration

Dream inspiration also played a significant part in research in the 1920s on the role of insulin in the human body. The Canadian physician Frederick Banting literally dreamed up the experimental technique that led him to establish the relationship between sugar and insulin. Even more remarkably, another dream led him to the idea that insulin extracted from animals could be used to treat human diabetes. Banting was awarded a Nobel Prize in 1923 for his life-saving achievements in medicine.

Another instance of unconscious problem solving led to a technological breakthrough at the laboratories of industrial giant DuPont. A researcher, Floyd Ragsdale, was developing machines to manufacture Kevlar fibre, used in bullet-proof vests. The equipment then used was unreliable and costly. Ragsdale had a dream about springs inserted into the tubes of the existing machines. He reported this to his boss, who was sceptical about the idea. Nevertheless, Ragsdale persisted and inserted springs into the tubes; the resulting equipment worked much better, and saved his company more than $3 million.

Dreams don't always provide the right answer first time. German physiologist Otto Loewi dreamed about an experiment with frogs that seemed to tell him that nervous impulses had a chemical rather than electrical basis. He awoke in the middle of the night and noted down his idea, but when he read it the next morning it made no sense. Fortunately, the next night the dream recurred; this time, he woke and went straight to the laboratory. The insight helped lead Loewi to the Nobel Prize for Medicine in 1936.

> "Let us learn to dream, gentlemen, then perhaps we shall find the truth. But let us beware of publishing our dreams till they have been tested by the waking understanding."
>
> Friedrich Kekulé, 19th-century chemist

Elias Howe

A new way to sew The development of the automatic sewing machine owes much to a dream had by American inventor Elias Howe (1819–1867). An ordinary sewing needle has its hole at the opposite end to the point, but Howe could not make this work when trying to automate the process. Then one night he dreamed about a tribe who threatened him with spears that had a loop just behind the spear head. He then saw the breakthrough of putting the hole near the tip of the needle.

Hidden abilities

One out of every two hundred people with autism have remarkable abilities. They can perform marvels of mental arithmetic or play accurately a tune they have heard only once. What is more, their abilities can help us to understand our own unconscious minds.

Charles is autistic. He has an IQ of around 58, and the reasoning skills of a four-year-old. He has severe problems dealing with other people, and needs to live in special accommodation. But he can do something few of the rest of us can do. Give him any date in this or the last century, and he can tell you on which day of the week it fell. Psychologist and autism expert Beate Hermelin recalls: 'When I first met Charles he was 13 years old and he immediately asked the date of my birthday. When I told him it was 7 August he said instantly, "That was on a Wednesday in 1940 and in 2004 it will be on a Wednesday again." I was stunned.'

Such 'savant abilities' are intriguing. How can they flourish in minds that otherwise seem so limited? Other autistic savants can accurately draw such complex buildings as London's St. Pancras Station from memory, or play a piece of music note-perfect after hearing it only once or twice. Because such remarkable skills stand out so dramatically, even scientists have tended to marvel at them and leave it at that. Explanations of how savants do it are usually in terms of memorising and constant practice. But it seems that something else is going on that may help us to understand our own minds better.

REMARKABLE ABILITIES

• Someone who is 70 years, 17 days and 12 hours old has been alive for 2,210,500,800 seconds. Peter, who is severely retarded, can work out such sums within half a minute.
• When autistic savant Paul was asked to play a 64-bar piece of music he had only heard twice, his version of the 798 notes was 92 per cent correct.
• The favourite activity of a pair of autistic savant twins, each with a mental age of nine, was to identify prime numbers of up to 20 digits long.

Unknown advantage In the 1988 film *Rainman* Dustin Hoffman plays an autistic savant whose gifts with numbers and playing cards included the ability to memorise phone books.

The unconscious in overdrive

Beate Hermelin suggests that autistic savants provide a glimpse of what happens when someone is totally governed by their unconscious abilities. Autistic savants are severely retarded but have one outstanding skill, which comes from one of the processing units in the unconscious brain working overtime. Hermelin argues that what autistic savants lack is a 'central executive' to pull their abilities together. This idea is backed up by recent research in Australia, which suggests that savants may have access to perceptual processing at a level of detail that, in most of us, is covered up by normal consciousness. Researcher Allan Snyder argues that normal consciousness is rather like the tip of an iceberg. Below the level of awareness are thousands of subsystems that process small units of information, which are in turn patched together to form a conscious perception. As the information is converted into conscious experience, our brains filter out a lot of unnecessary detail. The abilities of autistic savants may come about because their mode of information processing is not so overlaid by the 'higher' conceptual consciousness that most people bring to bear on their perceptions.

Meaning and consciousness

This focus on detail accounts for the problems that autistics encounter, as well as the talents of the savant minority. Typically, autistics have great difficulty seeing the wood for the trees. While the rest of us go for the 'gist' of things and can summarise the central points of something we have heard or seen, autistics concentrate on the details. The result is that they are often good at tasks that involve manipulating the parts of a whole, like the notes in a chord or the factors of large numbers.

A greater understanding of what is going on here comes from Hermelin's work with Christopher, who – although socially inept with a low IQ – knows 16 languages, including Finnish, Greek, Hindi and Welsh. His vocabulary is very impressive: in one test he learned 300 new words in Hebrew in five days after being shown them just once, but he falls down badly on grammar. 'His translations are usually word for word and he will often use English word-order when translating into other languages,' says Hermelin.

The significance of this is that, while we are all genetically programmed to learn grammar from a very early age, when we later learn a new language we have to learn the new grammatical rules consciously. Because Christopher's conscious thinking skills are so poor, he finds this almost impossible. Christopher's abilities are a good example of both the power of our unconscious processing abilities and their limitations. 'He doesn't use language to communicate or impart thoughts, like the rest of us,' says Hermelin. For Christopher, languages are simply a form of acquisition – a kind of linguistic stamp collecting. While the rest of us may lack Christopher's remarkable talents, our consciousness endows us with the precious ability to communicate with others.

> "Numbers are friends to me. It doesn't mean the same to you, does it, 3844? For you it is just a 3 and an 8 and a 4 and a 4. But I say hi, 62 squared."
>
> Wim Klein, autistic savant

DISCOVER YOUR HIDDEN THINKING POWERS

Conscious thinking is the surface layer of mind. Beneath it, the unconscious brain stores knowledge which, although it may not be consciously accessible, forms the source of our hunches and intuitions. 'Tuning in' to this knowledge involves circumventing the conscious mind and observing what emerges from the unconscious alone. Sometimes, of course, intuition should be overridden, because it is irrational and therefore can be misleading. It can also be counter-productive, urging us, for example, to flee from challenges. However, learning to interpret your inner voice can help you to sort useful intuitive guidance from beguiling nonsense.

TEST YOUR GUT FEELINGS

You may think that your feelings about future events are a good guide to how they are likely to turn out – but have you ever tested this? By checking the accuracy of your gut feelings, you can increase the value of the information they provide.

• Begin by noting any ordinarily inexplicable sensation, such as a shiver down your back, a 'lump' in the throat or butterflies in your stomach.

• Next, identify the emotion it signifies. Anticipation? Foreboding? Irritation? Try to match the sensation with a specific emotion.

• Work out what event the feeling relates to. This will be easy in some cases, but harder in others.

• Compare the outcome of the event to how you felt about it. If they match, be aware of that intuitive feeling when it next occurs, because it may accurately foretell your experiences. If they do not match, make a note of this. If the feeling recurs in relation to a similar event, you will know not to trust it.

TEASE OUT YOUR HIDDEN KNOWLEDGE

This is not a test of general knowledge or intelligence. Your unconscious mind knows how to decode the cryptic phrases on the right. The task is to let it come up with them. (Example: 4Q in a G means 4 quarts in a gallon.) See how many you can crack, then check the answers on page 159.

1) 7 W of the W
2) 26 L in the A
3) 24 H in a D
4) 12 S of the Z
5) 57 HV
6) 29 D in F in a LY
7) 2 BOTC
8) 10 GB (HOTW)
9) 9L of a C
10) 30 D has S

AVOIDING BAD DECISIONS

Intuition often causes people to make incorrect decisions because they unconsciously accept the way in which a choice is put to them. If this 'framing' is optimistic, they are more likely to accept whatever is being offered. In one study people presented with information framed in a positive way about a new medical drug were twice as likely to say they would take it as those receiving exactly the same information when this had been framed more negatively.

Whenever you are presented with information, to avoid being caught out unconsciously by the framing try turning it round to see if it can be presented in a different way. This is an occasion when the conscious mind should overrule its hidden partner.

GETTING IN THE FLOW

'Flow' is the brain state in which the unconscious mind gets on with the action while the conscious mind sits back and enjoys it. It is especially good for tasks that require integration of sensory skills with physical tasks, such as driving, dancing, painting or sculpting.
• Flow depends on losing awareness of the self, so harness yourself to the moment. If you fantasise about the future or recall the past, you will lose flow.
• Concentrate on what you are doing, not the way you do it. When practising a move in your favourite sport, imagine your limbs moving smoothly and accurately, but do not think about the movements you need to make.
• Relax. You can't work at achieving flow — it comes when you forget to try.

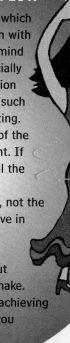

THE PILOT INSIDE

When you travel along a route, or around a town, much of the information you take in is laid down in a way that is not linked to words. If, later, you consciously try to remember the route you took, you might draw a blank.

This is because conscious memory tends to rely heavily on words for recall. However, if you simply head in the general direction of the place you are seeking, and go by 'feel', you might find that you get there without even trying.

RECOGNISING CONFLICT

Sometimes the conscious and unconscious minds give entirely conflicting guidance. When this happens, people often feel a sense of unease — the sense that perhaps something they are about to do is not quite right, or that what seems the 'obvious' choice could have a hidden catch. Once you learn to recognise the feeling of uncertainty that marks such conflicts of information, you can use it as a sign to pause, reflect, and — if possible — delay any decision until more information is available.

EYE TALK

Certain thoughts and feelings produce unconscious eye signals. For example, when a person is visualising something in their mind, their eyes will go up. You can use this knowledge to get on the same wavelength as the person you are talking to. It also gives you some idea of their train of thinking and whether they are tuning into what you are saying, or to their own inner thoughts.

Up and to the right or up and to the left
— visualising an imaginary scene or recalling a visual image. Staring straight ahead into the distance also indicates visualisation.

To the left side
— recalling speech

To the right and down
— feeling emotion

To the left and down
— internal dialogue

FREUD AND THE UNCONSCIOUS MIND

Freud did not invent the idea of the unconscious mind, but he certainly gave it substance and brought it to far wider attention. His work had a profound effect on society and there is no doubting his status as an intellectual giant of the 20th century. But what was it that led Freud to his revolutionary theories?

> **"A dream not interpreted is like a letter unread."**
>
> The Talmud

Freud's Vienna Freud founded his practice in Vienna in the 1880s. The Viennese bourgeoisie, from whom he drew most of his clients, were shocked by his insistence that sex lay at the root of neuroses.

Sigmund Freud was born in 1856 in the small town of Freiberg, Moravia, which today lies within the Czech Republic. His father, Jacob, was a wool merchant, and his mother, Amalia, was Jacob's second wife and nearly 20 years his junior. Freud grew up with seven younger siblings; he also had two half brothers, almost the same age as his own mother.

As a child, Freud was a voracious reader and was precociously intelligent: 'My Sigmund has more intelligence in his little toe than I have in my whole head,' said his father. Freud was driven to make his mark in the world not only by his innate intelligence but also by his status as a Jew attempting to forge a path into the European intellectual world. His early interest in science led him to medical school in Vienna, where he developed a passion for neurology and physiology, travelling to France to work with some of the foremost psychiatrists of the day.

Freud's early life provides some clues as to how he arrived at his theories of the mind. Freud's interest in family dynamics, which lies at the heart of his revolutionary ideas, was certainly triggered by observations of his own extended family. And his genius to connect diverse sources of information and so reveal hidden connections was strongly influenced by methods, including dream analysis, used in Judaism to interpret the scriptures.

Freud was initially fascinated by the use of hypnosis to treat hysteria and neurosis, and when he returned to Vienna from his studies with Charcot in Paris and Bernheim in Nancy, he opened a private practice in neuro-psychiatry with the help of his friend and collaborator, Josef Breuer.

Studies of hysteria

The seeds of Freud's understanding of the mind are seen in the case of 'Anna O', a woman treated by Breuer in the 1880s. Anna O presented a variety of hysterical symptoms, from minor headaches and lapses of concentration to hallucinations and paralysis of neck muscles. At one point in her treatment she displayed a fear of water and would not drink from a glass for some six weeks. When encouraged by Breuer to enter a hypnotic state, she recalled an incident in which an acquaintance allowed her dog to drink from a glass, an event Anna found disgusting. Immediately on coming round from the hypnotic state, she was fully able to drink normally. Evidently the memory of the dog episode had remained barred from normal consciousness, yet was responsible for her fear of drinking water. Merely recalling the memory was sufficient to let her overcome her fear. The 'talking cure' – psychoanalysis – was born.

Yet Freud felt there was something missing. Anna O's cure was piecemeal – there seemed more to her case than superficial symptoms, such as her inability to drink. Indeed, at the time that Breuer finished treating Anna, she began writhing with abdominal pain, displaying symptoms of a false pregnancy and declaring, 'Now comes Dr Breuer's child!' Freud surmised that Anna O's symptoms were caused by her sexual fantasies and frustrations, and this idea became the lynchpin of his later theories.

Real lives

THE CASE OF DORA

In 1900, an 18-year-old girl Freud referred to as 'Dora' was sent to him suffering from hysteria. Dora's father was having an affair with Frau K, a friend of the family. So that Frau K's husband would put up with this arrangement, Dora's father offered him Dora herself as a bribe. Dora told Freud of two occasions when Herr K had tried to collect on his end of the deal: both times, Dora rebuffed his advances.

In his analysis of Dora – and especially her dream images of a jewel box, which Freud equated with female genitalia – Freud postulated that Dora was unconsciously in love with her father, with Herr K and with Frau K. He read her disgust with Herr K's advances as a hysterical denial of her attraction. One of Dora's symptoms, a cough, was interpreted as an orgasm of the throat, associated with the desire to perform fellatio on her father.

Dora, however, rejected Freud's interpretations and ended the analysis after three months, whereupon Freud decided that she was revenging herself on him.

FOCUS ON FREUDIAN SLIPS

We have all experienced unconscious errors like slips of the tongue, mental blocks, or an inability to put a name to a familiar face. And we all make mistakes – indeed, fallibility is part of the human condition. But according to Freud, any slip, no matter how slight, reveals deeper issues in the mind. In his book *The Psychopathology of Everyday Life* (1904), Freud explored these errors, which he called parapraxes. For example, one Viennese gentleman reported to Freud that he had dined with an acquaintance tête à bête (head to fool) instead of tête à tête (head to head). To Freud, this slip was a channel through which the gentleman's real feelings emerged – he clearly thought his acquaintance to be a fool.

FACT: More books have been written on Freud, his ideas and the changes in society brought about by his work than any other 20th-century figure.

FOCUS ON

FREUD AND RELIGION

Freud saw psychoanalysis as a substitute for the self-cleansing imperative of religion. He referred to religion dismissively as 'the universal obsessional neurosis of humanity' and considered its rituals to be akin to the acts of someone who has not come to terms with an unconscious block.

To Freud, people of religious faith demonstrated a primitive form of thinking in which everything becomes submitted before an all-knowing father figure. He believed that men who had not resolved their Oedipus complex (by accepting the authority of their real father), were more susceptible to the acceptance of a 'super-father' – by which he meant God.

Sex and development

Freud saw all human behaviour as being motivated by unconscious drives to seek out food, water and, principally, sex. The motivational energy for these instincts he called libido (from the Latin for 'I desire'). He asserted (much to the disgust of contemporary society) that children go through several distinct stages of sexual development, and that adult neuroses are linked to repressed memories of these stages.

Freud noted that different parts of our bodies are the focus of tactile and sexual pleasure at different times of life. From birth to about 18 months, the mouth is the focus; from 18 months to 3 years, it is the anus; from 3 to 6 years, it is the genitalia. Freud named these stages oral, anal, and phallic, and recognised that each one included difficult transitions that could become the root of anxieties in later life.

A boy in the phallic stage, for example, seeks an external object for his phallic sexual desire. The obvious choice is his own mother, but there is one big obstacle to his plans – a sexual rival in the form of his father. The boy becomes jealous of his father and wishes him dead, but he feels sure that his father knows about his hostility. He believes that his father hates him, and will punish him by cutting off his penis. The boy's hatred and fear of his father escalates, until eventually he gives up on his mother as an object of desire. He begins to identify with his father, knowing that if he becomes like him, he too will one day enjoy a similar sexual partnership. Freud called this whole process the Oedipus complex after the character in Greek myth who murders his father and marries his mother.

According to Freud, unacceptable or taboo thoughts, memories and wishes (mainly about childhood sexual desires) are repressed or forced out of consciousness, but remain lodged in the unconscious. External events can trigger this material to emerge once more, causing the subject to relive the original anxiety. The thoughts are once again pushed back into the unconscious, resulting in constant conflict at the unconscious level.

Freud's structure of the mind

For Freud, the conflict is played out between three distinct aspects of the personality or foci of the mind – the id, ego and superego. These were famously described in his book *The Ego and the Id* (1925). The id is the source of our instinctive gratification-seeking drives. The ego is our general sense of identity, the 'I', that interacts with the world. The super-ego is a type of conscience, an internal reproduction of authority figures, especially our parents. The ego seeks to balance the demands of the id and the super-ego, while maintaining a healthy orientation to the real world.

In addition to these three foci, the mind comprises three regions: the conscious, the preconscious, and the unconscious. The Freudian unconscious is distinct from the conscious mind because of its sexual content and its illogicality. The preconscious includes material of which we are not

THE REGIONS OF THE MIND

Freud believed that, like an iceberg, most of the mind is submerged and inaccessible. He identified three regions: the conscious, the preconscious (or subconscious) and the unconscious. The regions are separate from, but related to, Freud's three aspects of personality: the id, the ego and the superego.

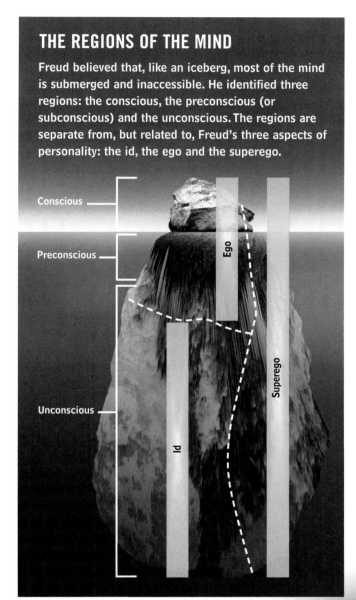

Conscious

Preconscious

Unconscious

Ego

Superego

Id

currently conscious, but that can enter consciousness with no limitations. Unconscious material is repressed – that is, it is actively barred from consciousness, and hence the ego may experience such material only in disguised form.

The talking cure

Perhaps the most important of Freud's assertions was that everything we think, say or do is driven by the unconscious; nothing occurs by chance. Psychoanalysis is a therapy that helps to uncover the hidden causes of our conscious thoughts and behaviour and so allows us to deal with the problems associated with repression. Its goal – according to Freud – is to make the unconscious become conscious. For example, when Anna O recalled the repressed memory of a dog drinking from a glass, it unblocked her own resistance to drinking.

Initially, Freud used hypnosis to examine his patients' unconscious material, but he gradually abandoned the technique because he felt that hypnosis was incapable of penetrating to the deepest – the sexual – aspects of a problem. He favoured the technique of free association, in which the patient would lie in a relaxed position on the famous couch and say whatever came into his or her head. Freud would then analyse what the patient had remembered – paying particular attention to symbols and fragments of dreams, which he considered to be 'the royal road to the unconscious'. The analyst – and only the analyst – could then determine what events in the patient's past had caused his or her current suffering.

Freud in London Freud left Vienna in 1938, following the occupation of the city by the Nazi regime. He and his youngest daughter Anna (an influential psychoanalyst in her own right) sought refuge in London. Freud was already in poor health and he died there in the following year.

Jung and the collective unconscious

Where Freud was the arch-detective of the unconscious, Carl Jung became its high priest. Influenced by myth and religion more than by scientific method, Carl Jung's influential ideas represent the farther reaches of psychology, at the boundary with mysticism.

The art of interpreting the unconscious reached new levels of sophistication in the work of Freud's one-time disciple, Carl Gustav Jung (1875–1961). Born in Switzerland, Jung studied medicine, specialising in the new discipline of psychiatry, and worked with psychotic patients in a mental hospital. Jung listened to his patients, trying to learn from their mental illness, and on reading Freud's great work, *The Interpretation of Dreams,* he recognised a kindred spirit – someone who tried to make sense of the irrational. The two met in 1907 and soon became great friends and intellectual collaborators.

At first, Jung agreed with Freud's theories on the unconscious, but soon he began to question his mentor's opinion that everything could be reduced to the sexual. Jung sought a broader context for the fundamental energy of the psyche, which eventually led him to value the spiritual quest as the primary means to psychic wholeness and general well-being.

To Freud, this was a heresy. Freud considered himself a scientist and even believed that his theories about the unconscious would be eventually substantiated by neurology. He could not countenance Jung's excursion into superstition, religion and spirituality, and the two great psychiatrists argued and became bitterly estranged.

> **"I have known, perhaps, an unusual number of those the world considered to be great, but Carl Gustav Jung is almost the only one of whose greatness I am certain."**
>
> Laurens van der Post

The structure of the unconscious

To Jung, the unconscious had two regions. One, the personal unconscious, was similar to Freud's notion – it was the storehouse of our repressed memories. The second was the collective unconscious, and this was Jung's own idea. This, he believed, contained the collective experience of all humanity – the instinctive behaviours, thoughts and fears inherited from our distant ancestors.

Jung's idea of the collective unconscious came from studying his patients' dreams and the widespread myths and traditions of humankind. He came to believe that certain key themes arose repeatedly in groups so diverse they could not have had direct contact. The ideas must therefore have arisen from some source to which all humans have access – a collective unconscious. One of his

Jung at his desk in 1952 Jung rejected Freud's view that dreams present our disguised sexual wishes, holding instead that they convey messages about what is lacking in our conscious lives.

The Mandala The essential structure of the mandala is a circle surrounding a square with a clearly demarcated centre. To Jung this symbolised the fourfold essence of the self (thinking, feeling, sensing and intuiting) in total balance. The most beautiful mandalas are ornate Tibetan forms that are used to aid meditation. The meditator identifies with the successive layers of the mandala from the outermost, said to represent the fire of mental activity, to the innermost, where the calm and wisdom of true being is found.

FACT: Jung coined the terms 'extravert' and 'introvert' – not to mean 'lively' and 'shy', as we use them today, but to indicate a person's orientation, either mainly to the outside world (extravert) or to the inner world (introvert).

patients, for example, dreamed of an erect phallus attached to the sun, where in the dream the wind arises. Jung found a similar idea in an ancient Mithraic liturgy, of which the patient could not have had any conscious knowledge.

Archetypes and individuation

Jung's notion of the collective unconscious comprised the archetypes – primary forms that direct the flow of images in the mind (rather like a magnet below a sheet controls an arrangement of iron filings on the surface). Jung maintained that the greatest challenge in our lives is to integrate the ideas welling up from the collective unconscious into our conscious lives. This process, which Jung called individuation, was for him a journey through which we encounter the archetypes. First, the 'shadow' archetype – aspects of ourselves that we unconsciously loathe or fear – must be recognised; second, in a man, the female aspects of the mind (the anima) must be integrated. As the journey continues, the individual encounters the deepest roots of human experience via the archetypes.

Jung also viewed symbols as access points for the archetypes. He considered a whole class of symbols to be 'unitive' – that is, expressing the urge of the psyche to unite opposites, especially its own conscious and unconscious realms. Jung regarded the mandala, which features prominently in Buddhist and Hindu traditions, as the most potent unitive symbol and as representing the self.

Jung's view of individuation was influenced by his study of the medieval practice of alchemy. Jung saw the alchemists' dream of turning base metals to gold as symbolising the quest to bring to fruition the true nature of our personality – the self, our inner gold.

SYNCHRONICITY

Jung led an extraordinary life of visions and seemingly telepathic experiences. In 1913, he had a vision of Europe being covered by a flood, the waters turning gradually to blood. Later, he interpreted this as a premonition of war.

Such events led Jung to argue that events may be connected via a non-causal principle he termed synchronicity. Jung further believed that there was meaning underlying synchronistic events (or coincidences), and understanding this meaning could provide a way to access the unconscious. Accordingly, he became fascinated by divination, astrology and similar practices, which he felt could yield insights into his patients' inner minds.

THE PSYCHOANALYTIC LEGACY

> "Like an Old Testament prophet, Freud undertook to overthrow false gods, to rip the veils away from a mass of dishonesties and hypocrisies, mercilessly exposing the rottenness of the contemporary psyche."
>
> Carl Jung

Although psychologists now think that Sigmund Freud was wrong about many things, there is no denying that he had a huge influence on Western culture, as have many psychoanalysts who followed him. Without Freud, we might still be living in the buttoned-up world of Victorian values.

Over the past twenty years, scientific psychology has established beyond doubt the key importance of the brain's unconscious processing. We know that conscious experience rests on a base of unconscious processes in perception, memory and emotion. But today's ideas are a long way from Freud. In the words of neuropsychologist John Kihlstrom, Freud's model of the unconscious was 'hot and wet; it seethed with lust and anger; it was hallucinatory, primitive and irrational'. None of these characteristics is evident in the unconscious of scientific psychology today.

Evaluating Freud

Should we, then, cast Freud into the waste-bin? Are his ideas hopelessly outdated? Many have dismissed his work on the grounds that his methods were suspect, his hypotheses were vague and untestable, and he was notoriously selective in what he chose to include in his published work. But Freud deserves a more subtle evaluation; he gave us a way of viewing ourselves that goes beyond consideration of verifiable facts. Freud was a key figure in changing society, and we probably would not want to turn the clock back to the pre-Freudian world of Victorian propriety. He opened the way to us being more conscious of ourselves and exploring our own

(F)OCUS ON   D.H. LAWRENCE AND THE PSYCHOANALYSTS

Love and sex are the powerful recurring themes in Lawrence's work. In his famous semi-autobiographical novel, *Sons and Lovers*, an almost erotic bond develops between the central character, Paul Morel, and his mother, evoking the Freudian idea of the Oedipus complex.

However, in many ways, Lawrence's understanding of human consciousness was closer to Jung's view than to that of Freud. Like Jung, Lawrence emphasised the joining of opposites in order to realise a higher inner nature. Such a union, he believed, could be achieved through sex. 'Sex is our deepest form of consciousness,' wrote Lawrence. 'It is utterly non-ideal, non-mental. It is pure blood-consciousness.'

By setting these ideas within the lives of powerful, believable characters in his fiction, Lawrence vitalised them as much as, if not more than, any of the analysts.

minds. Without Freud, it is unlikely that the concept of openness, so central to psychotherapy, would have taken such root in our culture.

Freud was also factually correct in regarding the unconscious as much more extensive than consciousness. His view that unconscious mental activity deals with multiple meanings of words or images is quite consistent with modern experimental findings. Indeed, psychologists agree that what differentiates unconscious from conscious activity is the ability of the former to operate in parallel mode, rather than in a serial fashion.

So where was Freud wrong? In a word – sex. There is, for example, no good evidence for the existence of anything remotely like the Oedipus complex (see page 88). Moreover, feminists have correctly argued that his theories are hopelessly male-orientated. Freud's supposed female equivalent of the Oedipus complex – the Electra complex – is poorly thought out and, again, lacking any reasonable evidence. All one can say in Freud's defence is that he so shocked society that he forced a change towards a more liberal stance in which sexual matters could at least be aired.

Evaluating Jung

Jung too exerted a powerful influence on society, especially in the area of religion. Jung felt that the religion of his day had become sterile and largely divorced from people's real experience. Through his concept of individuation, he revitalised what it means to embark on a spiritual journey, but at the cost of 'psychologising' religion. For Jung, God could be understood only as a reality of the psyche – the god within. This is hardly the traditional God that inspires the devotions of the faithful, and some have therefore criticised Jung for creating a self-centred form of religion – religion for the 'me-generation'.

Like Freud, Jung's claims to the scientific validity of his theories are also doubtful, and there is little evidence to back up many of his ideas. For example, the existence of a collective unconscious is claimed from the uniformity of most people's experience with hallucinogenic drugs. Medicine men from a tribe in South America use hallucinogenic plants to enter a visionary world in which they encounter powerful animals, especially snakes and birds of prey. When the drug is given to Westerners with no knowledge of the tribe's customs and expectations, they may experience similar animal hallucinations – evidence, say Jungian researchers, that the images spring from a collective source. Evidence like this is at best equivocal, and hardly a sufficient basis for the theory it is said to support.

Common symbols Cave art from prehistory to recent times shows striking similarities, whether from Europe, Asia or, as this image, from Australia. This lends support to Jung's idea that certain symbols are common to all humanity.

THINK AGAIN!

ARCHETYPAL POPSTARS

The Beatles were loved for their music. But perhaps – just perhaps – their appeal also drew on the archetypes of Jungian theory. Some Jungians maintain that The Beatles represented four archetypes – the philosopher-king, the eternal youth, the mystic and the trickster. By this theory, the Beatles tapped the collective unconscious, releasing its energy to creative effect and empowering us through our own psyches. Or maybe they just wrote good tunes!

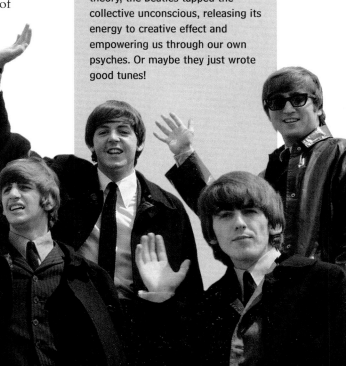

(F) CUS ON

HOLLYWOOD AND THE UNCONSCIOUS

In 1957, America was gripped by the case of Ed Gein, a farmer who had murdered some twenty women. Gein dragged their dead bodies home to keep his mother company – his dead mother, that is, whose body he had propped up in a chair in the farmhouse so that he could talk to her. The story inspired Alfred Hitchcock to create *Psycho*. The director also knew his Freud and placed emphasis on the Oedipal aspect of the son–mother relationship. Hitchcock drew on Freud again for the dream sequence in *Spellbound,* which was designed with Salvador Dali's help.

George Lucas in 1977 began the blockbuster *Star Wars* series, shaping characters by Jungian archetypes. For the hero Luke, the shadow archetype is represented by Darth Vader. The fact that he is Luke's father adds an extra emphasis to Luke's battle to overcome his shadow. Princess Leia is an anima figure (the female aspect), and the integration of this archetype occurs when Luke realises that she is his twin sister. And the wise old man archetype is portrayed by Yoda, the Jedi master.

Cultural catalyst

Freud's most important work, *The Interpretation of Dreams,* was published in 1900, the same year that a crucial paper appeared by the physicist Max Planck, which in turn led Einstein to develop his theories. The word 'relativity' could be said to capture the essence of the early 20th century. Freud should be credited with the important role he played in ushering in the new perspective, which allowed ideas of absolute, God-given morality to be challenged, and the rigid roles occupied by men and women in society to be displaced. Although moves in these directions preceded Freud, his view of the mind encouraged their growth.

Freudian ideas fell on ground already prepared, which is why they spread like wildfire in the early years of the new century. Artists and writers were strongly influenced by Freud and the 'discovery' of the unconscious. In his 1924 *Surrealist Manifesto*, André Breton praised him for shining a light into what Breton regarded as the most important part of the mind, the unconscious. Surrealism rejected the logic and rationalism of the conscious, preferring to explore the irrational world legitimised by Freud. Freud himself was sceptical of the surrealist movement but was impressed by Salvador Dali, whose technical mastery he respected. There is no mistaking the Freudian ideas of dream work in Dali's pictures, with their distortion of images, condensation of ideas and blurring of meaning.

The idea of an unconscious hopelessly dominated by base and self-centred needs appears in many literary works of a similar time. Joseph Conrad's *Heart of Darkness* aligns the disturbing colonial world in the African Congo with the evil and corrupting unconscious of man, showing not so much the direct influence of Freud as the effect of his ideas filtering through the cultural world. And D.H. Lawrence drew more explicitly on psychoanalytic ideas in his work; his classic novel *Sons and Lovers* explores the Oedipal attraction between son and mother.

Therapy after Freud

Despite Freud's great influence, his approach to therapy was considered too narrow by many of his followers. First Jung, then the Austrian psychologist Alfred Adler, felt that Freud's insistence on sexual theory was detrimental to analysis. Adler believed that the will to power was a central motive for our actions, and his therapy was directed to understanding how our feelings of inferiority could be overcome. The German-born psychoanalyst and social philosopher Erich Fromm emphasised the social origin of inner conflicts, and felt that understanding the way in which we establish relationships should be a central theme of therapy.

Similar ideas are found in the influential 'object relations' school, which stresses the importance of early relationships. Someone who experiences a problematic childhood, in which secure bonds to early carers are not well established, will suffer not only in their later interactions with other people but also in their involvement with 'objects' in their environment. To cite one example, they may be more likely to become entangled with drug

abuse because the object – the drug – is imbued with the character of a relationship: it is rewarding and damaging at the same time.

Over recent years, therapy and counselling have developed into a huge industry. Freud has been interpreted less rigidly, sometimes with only token adherence to his key notion that unconscious meanings developed in the past can exert critical effects on the present. And the image of the therapist as the sole wise interpreter of hidden motives has waned. In the influential client-centred therapy developed by American psychologist Carl Rogers, the therapist concentrates on creating an aura of trust, in which the 'client' can move towards solving his or her own problems. The therapist does not interrupt and rarely offers advice. While this move away from the authoritarian character of Freudian analysis is generally accepted as an improvement, perhaps a sense of plumbing the full depths of the mind has been lost along the way.

Surrealist influence The work of Salvador Dali, such as *The Metamorphosis of Narcissus* (1937), was strongly influenced by Freud's ideas of the unconscious mind.

PIONEERS
JACQUES LACAN – REINTERPRETING FREUD

The French psychoanalyst Jacques Lacan (1901–1981) was probably the most influential of Freud's reinterpreters. Early in his career he was expelled from the International Psychoanalytic Association for his unorthodox approach. But this probably says more about how most psychoanalysts after Freud had turned his ideas into a dogma than it does about Lacan's supposed errors. Where Freud had argued that the ego strives to relate to the real world (the reality principle), Lacan taught that egohood is a fiction, a construct of language. As such it is the 'human being's mental illness'. The purpose of entering into dialogue with the unconscious is not to bring about healing, but to approach what Lacan calls 'The Real', an ungraspable realm of experience beyond language. Given the unknowability of 'The Real', there is no end to the psychoanalytic process – only the journey.

EXPLORING YOUR UNCONSCIOUS MIND

Just as the stars cannot be seen during the day because they are obscured by the stronger light of the sun, so too with the unconscious mind: it is ever-present, but its activity is obscured by the light of consciousness. Penetrating the unconscious involves learning to be attentive in a defocused way. You must allow what arises simply to be, without rushing to hasty conclusions, and accept that there is a source of knowledge within, for belief in the workings of the unconscious is the key that turns the lock.

FREE ASSOCIATION

Freud believed that free association was a useful way to tap into the unconscious mind. If you have (or can borrow) a tape recorder with a microphone, you can try this for yourself.

Begin by choosing a fragment of material – a word, an idea, a feeling or a picture in your mind. The origin of the fragment is not important: it may have surfaced during a dream or emerged spontaneously from your imagination. When you have chosen a fragment, hold it in mind and talk out loud, recording what you say. Say whatever comes into your head in response to the fragment. Remember there is no right or wrong, only that which flows. If a picture arises in your mind, let visualisation take over as the focus for your associations. If the flow dries up, try to find ways round it: it may feel like a door that won't open – if so, look for an exit to the side.

When you have finished, play back the tape and think about the associations you have made. Try to interpret the words and images in relation to your own life – your parents, your childhood, significant people and events in your life, and your hopes and fears.

FOOD FOR THOUGHT

The role of food in our lives goes far beyond simple nourishment, and our attitudes towards it are deeply significant. This is not surprising, since food does, after all, enter our insides – our inner being. According to Freud, the oral stage of infancy could determine features of our later life. And eating disorders can be especially problematic around adolescence, the time when a person's orientation to the world beyond their family is being established.

So what does food mean to you? Is it something to be savoured or rushed? Then there is the matter of specific foods. Cast your mind back to a meal that has stayed strongly in your memory. Who were you with, or what was the occasion? Which food item really stands out? Free associate around that item, or an item you really don't like. When did you first realise your distaste for it? What is its significance? Honest attention to your associations can be especially revealing in this area.

DREAMING AND KNOWING

Freud said that dreams are the 'royal road to the unconscious'. Using dreams to access the unconscious needs long-term commitment, but can be rewarding. If you want to give it a try, you will need to record your dream life systematically, so keep a diary and a pen next to your bed. When going to sleep, hold the intention in mind that you will write down your dreams; sometimes, it helps to visualise yourself sitting up and writing in the diary. Whenever you awake with a dream fragment in mind – even in the middle of the night – resist the temptation to go back to ` sleep: sit up and write it down.

Examine your diary daily and at longer intervals, perhaps monthly. In your daily review, identify any content that relates to events that happened in the last few days. Spotting this 'day residue' is not normally too hard, but sometimes the material may be disguised, so you may need to associate around the images to discern their relevance. Mark the day residue passages in your diary, then when you look at it monthly you will be able to see more clearly the patterns that go beyond daily processing. Sometimes these will be recurring themes, sometimes developing patterns or unfolding stories. Don't seek obvious interpretations. The objective is more to develop a close relationship with your unconscious, and trite answers (such as 'the woman with the dark coat is my mother') can block that relationship. Instead, look for ways to amplify the images. For example, if there is a character in your dream diary that you do not immediately recognise, try to visualise them and have imaginary conversations with them. What do they tell you? You may eventually reach a stage where you can consciously engage with the dream content while you are dreaming (see pages 58–59). Again, setting the intention prior to falling sleep is important. You will be surprised what you can achieve.

THE WORD AT THE CENTRE

This exercise uses cues from words in the conscious mind as a way to access material in the unconscious mind. Write eight words across the top of a sheet of paper – they can be any eight words, but they should not make a sentence. Then write another eight words at the bottom. Return to the top and think of a word that somehow connects the first two words on the sheet. For example, if these words were 'tree' and 'mud', you might choose 'root' as the connecting word. Go on to the next two words, and continue making these connections, working row by row alternately from the top and the bottom of the page. Eventually you will end up with one final word in the centre (see the diagram below as a guide). What does that central word mean to you? Spend some time contemplating that word – it will be significant!

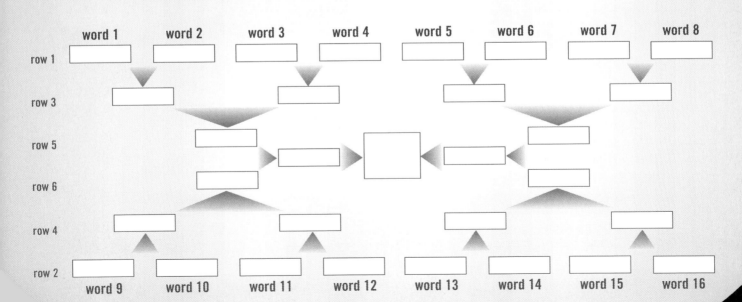

TRUTHFUL SLIPS

Freud believed that any slip of the tongue had meaning and unmasked a hidden motive. Few psychologists today would go so far, but it is true that slips of the tongue can sometimes reveal unconscious thoughts and may be worth examining. When you make a verbal slip, consider how and when it happened. If a word was simply mispronounced, it may not be significant. But if the slip was accompanied by an emotional response – perhaps a rush of energy, or a shiver – no matter how slight, then it could be worth exploring. What significance does the word hold for you? Free associating around this word may help uncover this, and help reveal what your unconscious is trying to tell you.

If you reflect on your verbal slips, you'll also become aware of how ideas that concern you sometimes break out in speech, despite your conscious intentions. This can often be enlightening, but also uncomfortable. Take this case. Daniel meets a friend who has just separated from her husband. He knows about her situation, but decides not to mention it directly. She asks Daniel to light her cigarette, so he tries to strike a match, but presses too hard and snaps it. Without thinking, he exclaims, 'It's a pain when your match breaks, isn't it?' It's likely that his choice of words comes as much from awareness of his friend's problematic private life as from the broken matchstick.

ACTIVE IMAGINATION

Jung used the term 'active imagination' for the process we need to cultivate to understand the unconscious. It involves letting ideas unfold without interference. This sounds easy, but it is probably one of the hardest things for us to achieve because consciousness usually cannot help but interfere. One way to try to engage active imagination is to take some clay or plasticine and mould it in your hands. Let shapes arise spontaneously, rather than deliberately trying to make a particular object. When it feels as if a satisfactory shape has emerged, leave it. Don't even think about it for a day or more. Then return to your shape and consider what it represents. Think especially of creatures or scenes you may have encountered in stories, myths or films. What does it tell you about yourself?

A TUNE IN YOUR HEAD

Whenever you notice that a song is playing in your mind, ask yourself why. If you have just heard the tune on the radio, then it probably has no deep significance. But there are many times when you find yourself humming a tune or holding a song in your head, without any obvious, conscious reason. In these cases, examine your associations to the tune. What is its title? Where did you hear it? Who were you with? What message does it hold for you now? For example, if you find the song 'Strawberry Fields' stuck in your head, you could be remembering a time when you were told off for spilling a bowl of strawberries – and this memory may have been triggered by a current criticism.

PSYCHOLOGICAL TYPES

Jung believed that human behaviour is not random, but follows identifiable patterns that develop from the structure of the human mind. He argued that personality could be classified according to the style of thinking we employ when we perceive and when we judge.

Jung argued that there are basic functions underlying personality – thinking, feeling, perceiving and intuiting – any one of which can be dominant in any individual. He combined these basic functions with his concepts of the introvert and extravert, giving eight basic different types of personality.

To find out which you are, consider how you go about redecorating, for example. Do you think it through, perhaps considering what's in vogue at present (thinking)? Are you mainly influenced by the aesthetics of colour and pattern combinations (perceiving)? Does it have to feel pleasant (feeling)? Or, perhaps, you can't really explain it, but it just 'clicks' when it's right (intuiting). The polar opposite (thinking opposite to feeling; perceiving opposite to intuition) to your dominant function represents an underdeveloped potential, and can help to explain tendencies in behaviour. You may find it irritating, for example, if your partner operates mainly from the opposite function. You may gain insight into your interactions if, instead of merely reacting, you examine the cause of the irritation, and think about the dominant and opposite functions in your and your partner's personalities.

TRUE LIFE DRAMA

Jung believed that the unconscious mind of all human beings contains templates of behaviour called archetypes. According to Jung, these archetypes also appear in the myths and legends of all cultures. Reflecting on mythology can help you to discover which archetypes are most prominent in your unconscious, and thus reveal something of your unconscious motives.

When you read a myth, story or fairytale, ask yourself which ones have most resonance with you. Which characters and situations do you respond to most strongly? The neglected stepchild, the embattled hero, the imprisoned princess?

Another way to find your links to mythology is to try to create a drama from your own life. Write down the details of your childhood, your youth, and your working life. What seems to be the principal direction of your life's journey? You will find that there are crucial moments when major directions were established – it may have been a house move in childhood, the decision of what to study at university, a chance encounter on a holiday, or choosing to change jobs. In retrospect, you will see that there are important moments that shaped the course of your life. Focus on those moments and see which mythic, or perhaps biblical, characters could be related to them. It might be that, like Atlas, you feel you have the weight of the world on your shoulders; or perhaps the occasion when the biblical Joseph is sold into slavery by his brothers has some meaning for you. A myth is an exploration of just these kinds of 'big' human moments. Just as the mythic character is engaged on some form of challenging path, so too are you.

4 CONSCIOUSNESS AND OURSELVES

The sense of self that pervades our consciousness is as natural to us as breathing. Yet unlike the act of breathing, which we know is the function of the lungs, there is no specific part of the body or brain that we can pinpoint as the generator of this sense of personal self. So how does it come about? How is the unending stream of disparate thoughts and impressions that crowd our consciousness distilled into a coherent, enduring sense of self?

Perhaps surprisingly, researchers have found that it is not something we are born with: rather, it is one of the attributes of mind that children develop as they mature. And while the pace of development may slow down, the maturing of personal consciousness is a lifelong process.

Our sense of self at any age depends strongly on our interactions with others, and these can take place at an unconscious as well as conscious level. In many ways these interactions provide the basis of our identity – an identity that lives on, in the minds of those we have known and loved, when our own life comes to an end.

IDENTITY AND THE STREAM OF CONSCIOUSNESS

Consciousness is inherently individual. It is not simply experiencing – there is always a 'me' at the centre doing the feeling, responding and interpreting. But locating this self has proved surprisingly difficult.

Towards the end of the 19th century, pioneering psychologist William James began an exhaustive labour of introspection – a search for the core of his consciousness. But no matter how hard he tried and no matter how complex his mental gymnastics, James could find no centre – no thinker doing the thinking. His thoughts seemed to flicker and play of their own accord, some temporarily illuminated by the spotlight of attention, others dancing on the fringes. And even to observe his thoughts, James realised, was only to have thoughts about thoughts. His mind was an ever-changing play of mental events and, it appeared, his notion of a self was an illusion.

James found a resolution to this existential crisis by likening consciousness to a tumbling stream. The waters of a stream are always in flux, never in precisely the same state twice. For every big eddy – for every distinct thought or clear impression – there are many more background ripples and swirls. But the stream itself has a history, a continuous identity behind the superficial play of the current. Gradually the waters etch out their own banks, creating a landscape that in turn shapes the flows of the water.

> **"As the brain changes are continuous, so do all consciousnesses melt into each other like dissolving views."**
>
> William James, from *Principles of Psychology* (1890)

The self can be seen in the same way. It is not an inner observer that is a target for mental experiences. Instead, it is the vessel that gives shape to these experiences. From birth, the brain accumulates memories and habits, which in turn shape its circuitry and processing paths, and so guide its response to each subsequent moment. This is what makes every person's consciousness unique and individual. Each brain becomes the product of its own singular history.

Shaping the mind

For a long time, James's insight was lost to science. In the middle decades of the 20th century, consciousness was viewed as a software program running on a generalised machine, so the sense of self was merely the sum of many processing events. Memories, for example, were called up by processing – they did not do the processing. But more recent and realistic models of the brain fit well with James's analogy. Today, many scientists view the brain as a neural network, where webs of connections develop through experience, and where the nature of our consciousness arises from our specific history of interactions with the world. And a new generation of computers can also be shaped by their 'life story', with their own unique patterns of processing formed during a 'training' phase.

PIONEERS   *WILLIAM JAMES*

Although written over 100 years ago, the works of William James (1842–1910) are still valued for helping to illuminate human thought processes. James, whose brother was the novelist Henry James, had a privileged but odd upbringing, his father trailing the family around the world in pursuit of the perfect education. James gained a degree in medicine from Harvard University in 1869, while also reading widely in psychology and philosophy, and set up the first-ever psychology course there in the 1870s. Although never quite capturing the public imagination like Freud, James's insights were highly influential. Authors such as James Joyce and Virginia Woolf tried to recreate in words James's metaphor of consciousness as a flow of images, urges and snatches of inner speech. Joyce's *Ulysses* became the classic 'stream of consciousness' novel. In this extract, Leopold Bloom listens to a singer in a bar:

'Glorious tone he has still. Cork air softer also their brogue. Silly man! Could have made oceans of money. Singing wrong words. Wore out his wife: now sings. But hard to tell. Only the two themselves. If he doesn't break down. Keep a trot for the avenue. His hands and feet sing too. Drink. Nerves overstrung. Must be abstemious to sing. Jenny Lind soup: stock, sage, raw eggs, half pint of cream.'

A sense of self

So is our sense of self simply the feeling of being the sum of our histories? James realised that our self-sense is not quite this passive. Aspects of our identity are actively constructed. For a start, there is our somatic self – the feeling of what it is like to inhabit our own skins. One of the main tasks of the brain is to draw up the mental boundaries that divide the 'me' from the 'not-me'. Just ponder the feat of being able to chew food in the cramped confines of your mouth. Tongue and dinner move in all directions and yet we manage to keep ourselves separate from our meals and avoid biting ourselves while chewing. The brain's construction of such boundaries is precise, yet also elastic. A racing car driver will feel his tyres gripping on tight corners as if they were an extension of his body, and hammers, pens and paintbrushes can come to feel like part of the hand if used for long periods of time.

Social consciousness

Another aspect of our sense of self derives from the fact that we are social creatures. We must take into account other consciousnesses – the people around us. The more we are aware of the mental existence of others, the more aware we are of our own mental existence. So while the self requires a brain, it has no actual anatomical location. It is rooted in our relationships with our physical space, our social space, and our personal histories.

> **"No man steps into the same river twice."**
>
> Heraclitus (540–480 BC)

FOCUS ON

COGNITIVE DISSONANCE

Consciousness is full of conflicting knowledge and urges, and we often act without fully understanding the reasons why. However, we like to see ourselves as consistent and in control. Psychologists have a term to describe the urge to paper over the cracks in the facade of the self: cognitive dissonance.

If you bought an expensive car and then found that it is uncomfortable on long drives, would you decide to get rid of the car, or console yourself by appreciating its firm, race-bred, handling? Or perhaps you are a smoker and see the latest lung cancer statistics. Do you give up smoking, or tell yourself that as you are only a relatively light smoker you are probably not going to be susceptible to cancer anyway?

Because of the need to see ourselves as unified in mind, most of us become quite skilled at justifying whatever it is that we find our 'selves' deciding to do.

MULTIPLE IDENTITIES

A killer claims he is innocent because his 'alter ego' did it. A woman tells a psychiatric conference she is inhabited by more than 180 different personalities. If these reports are true, then the human mind is – astonishingly – able to host not just one self, but many.

"They cope with the pain and horror of the abuse they suffered by dividing it up into little pieces and storing it in such a way that it's hard to put back together and hard to remember."

Frank Putnam, psychiatrist

The 19th-century thinker William James argued that our sense of self is glued together by the stream of consciousness (see page 102). Is it possible that, under certain circumstances, the 'glue' could disintegrate and allow two or more selves to inhabit the same mind? Some psychiatrists think so, and label the resulting bizarre state multiple personality disorder; others see it as a fake or delusion. But before examining the arguments, consider the classic case of 'Julia'.

During therapy, Julia described how she had been 'losing' chunks of time since she was a child. She once came round in an unfamiliar classroom and could not account for the last two years. Another time she found herself in a seedy bar talking to a man who seemed to know her much better than she knew him. It emerged that during the 'lost' periods, Julia had been displaced by one of her other selves, and these alternative personalities began to take shape. Among them was George, the burly protector; Joanne, the playful 12-year-old; Sandi, the terrified four-year-old; and Elizabeth, the administrator, who kept some order among the other personalities. In all, Julia had nearly 100 selves.

As therapy progressed, it seemed that the splits in Julia's personality had been caused by a childhood of extreme physical and sexual abuse. Julia had contained her memories of trauma by dividing them among a cast of characters; through therapy she was apparently able to make herself whole again.

Products of therapy?

But can the self really disintegrate under such pressure, or is multiple personality just a product of therapy itself, as patients respond to the suggestions of their counsellors? It is certainly a fact that there had been very few reports of multiple personality until 1973,

FACT FILE   FAMOUS CASES OF MULTIPLE PERSONALITIES

• An early case of multiple personality emerged in 1906. Christine Beauchamp (real name Clara Fowler) sought help for neurotic symptoms. Under hypnosis, a flirtatious alter ego called Sally emerged first. Later came an angry child-like figure dubbed the Devil or the Idiot.

• In the 1950s, a demure 25-year-old telephonist named Eve White (real name Christine Sizemore) was referred to Dr Corbett Thigpen complaining of headaches, blackouts and hearing voices. Hypnosis revealed Eve Black, a provocative alter ego. Later came Jane, a calm and mature personality, and a further 19 personalities. The case inspired the celebrated book *The Three Faces of Eve*, which was made into a film with Joanne Woodward (right).

• Also in the 1950s, a young student called Sybil Dorsett (real name Shirley Mason) entered therapy, and a tale of abuse by her schizophrenic mother emerged. Under hypnosis, Sybil revealed 16 different personalities.

MULTIPLE PERSONALITY CASES IN COURT

Multiple personality disorder, both faked and apparently real, has featured in several notable court cases. In 1979, Kenneth Bianchi, the 'Hillside Strangler', was charged with the rape and murder of two girls in Los Angeles. Bianchi said that his alter ego, Steve, who emerged during therapy, was to blame, conveniently getting Bianchi off the hook. But when Bianchi was examined by a more critical psychiatrist, Bianchi's apparent symptoms were found to be at odds with clinical knowledge of multiple personality disorder. It was concluded that Bianchi was faking and he was sentenced to life imprisonment.

A case where multiple identities provided a basis for prosecution was heard in 1995. Two women with the disorder had their alter egos sworn in to give evidence against their psychiatrist. The courts upheld their claims that the psychiatrist had sexually abused the alter egos during therapy, swearing them to secrecy.

when the best-selling book *Sybil* related the story of a woman with 16 alter egos. Rates of diagnosis rocketed after its publication, leading doubters to say that this was proof of an imagined syndrome. But those who believe the syndrome is real say that it only shows that therapists now know what to look for.

It is also a fact that there is a consistent pattern to the disorder, which lends weight to the opinion that the multiple personalities are real. Sufferers tend to have a high IQ; there are usually recognisable types among the alter egos; and behind practically every case there lies a tale of extreme and prolonged childhood abuse. Importantly, the abuse has to happen during early childhood – trauma even in teenage years does not produce the disorder.

Open to suggestion?

It is possible that children, who have still-growing brains and incompletely integrated personalities, could be prone to deep-rooted splits in which alternative selves grab a share of the same brain. While doubters concede that most sufferers have been abused, they argue that this fact is significant only because it leads them to seek therapy. Once in therapy, their unstable mental health makes them vulnerable to suggestion. The doubters add that people with multiple personalities almost always score very high for hypnotisability (see page 46). It could be that the hypnosis routinely used to get to the cause of the symptoms is in fact producing them.

It is probably too extreme to claim that all multiple personalities are produced on the therapist's couch. However, people who are highly hypnotisable and who thus have an ability to dissociate (to separate themselves from reality) might be expected to use this skill to escape genuine abuse during childhood. Therapy may contribute to an elaboration of the personalities, but the initial splitting – the act of dissociation – probably takes place at the moment of abuse, just as the sufferers report.

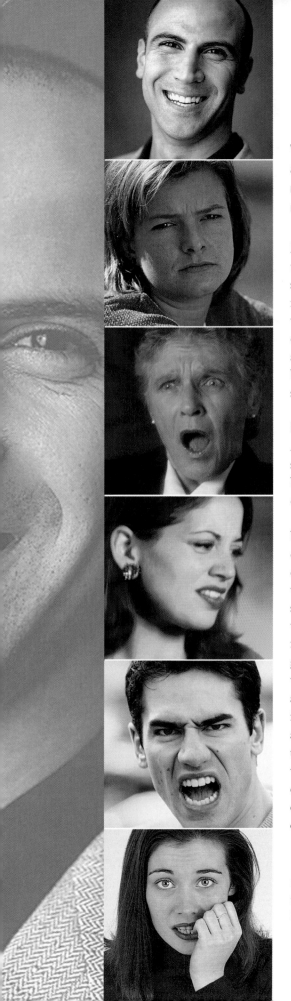

BODY LANGUAGE

When we interact with others, we convey a great deal of information about ourselves through our body language. Such non-verbal signals may be quite unwitting – although the thoughts and attitudes they reflect are often all too conscious.

Much of the information that we get from body language is picked up unconsciously. We are often unable to identify quite why, after being with someone, we have been left with a particular impression of his or her mood. We might just say 'I felt he was upset', without being able to say what has led us to this conclusion. Similarly, we all give out signals that offer clues to our own mood without generally being aware of what we are doing. Some of these signals – such as many facial expressions – are so basic that they go back to a time before humans had language; others simply accompany our verbal utterances, adding to their meaning.

Body movement and speech

As we speak, we cannot help but move. Body movement is closely synchronised with speech – not just our hand gestures, but all parts of the body. Even movements of the legs and the feet have been shown to be co-ordinated with speech.

This language of the body is both highly visible and silent. This can make it extremely useful. We can catch or hold people's attention with flamboyant gestures; we can stress important words or phrases with a movement of the head, a raised eyebrow or an emphatic gesture. Just as a picture may be worth a thousand words, so miming an action may have much greater impact or be more informative than a long verbal description. Some things are too delicate to put into words, but you may be able to express what you mean just with an appropriate hand movement or facial expression. Sometimes we don't want to put something into words for other people to hear, but because body language is silent, it is possible to

> **"Body language adds emphasis to what we say, while the words we use refine the meaning of our body language."**
>
> Peter Bull, psychologist and body language expert

Universal language These six facial expressions are believed to be understood by all humans independent of their culture. From the top: happiness, sadness, surprise, disgust, anger, fear.

catch someone's eye or exchange a meaningful glance so that he or she gets the message.

How we mean others to take our remarks can also be conveyed through body language. What is intended as a joke may be indicated by a smile – and if you say something with a smile, you can get away with almost anything! Conversely, in deadpan humour, nonverbal indicators are withheld; deadpan achieves its effect because we are never quite sure how seriously it should be taken.

Emotions and body language

The 'body language' of the face is of prime importance in communicating emotion. Even newborn babies are capable of producing virtually all the facial movements of an adult. At least six facial expressions of emotion are thought to be universal: happiness, sadness, surprise, disgust, anger and fear are recognised in much the same way by members of different cultures throughout the world. The ability to make and recognise these expressions seems to be genetically programmed into us.

While spontaneous expressions are almost certainly innate – and are a vital source of information about the feelings of others – posed expressions are learned. This idea is supported by the observation that children who are born blind show the same range of spontaneous facial expressions as do sighted children, but they are less able to pose expressions of common emotions. This may be because they lack appropriate feedback on how well they are doing – just as people who are born deaf cannot easily learn to sing.

Once we learn to have some control over our facial expressions, we can conceal what we feel and even fake an expression of the opposite emotion. Some people are much better at this than others. There are those whose faces are an 'open book' and others who conceal emotion behind a 'poker face'. Studies of gender differences show that women tend to express their feelings more openly than men. Cultural differences also affect the display of emotion. Traditionally in Japan there has been a taboo against the expression of negative emotions (such as anger) in public, whereas no such taboo exists in the USA. This can lead to difficulties in communication between people of different cultures if one is more expressive than another.

There are also significant differences between individuals when it comes to picking up signals from facial expressions. Some people are very perceptive, others much less so. Tests have been devised to assess nonverbal perceptiveness: where a gender difference is found, it invariably favours women. This perhaps is the foundation for women's fabled intuition.

Deadpan humour Silent movie comedian Buster Keaton (shown here in a scene from *The General*, 1926) was a master of deadpan humour, betraying no emotion even in the most drastic situation.

Focus on

VOICE MATCHING

Matching your speech style to that of someone you are speaking to is the verbal equivalent of mirroring body language. Its effect is to build harmony between you and the other person. It entails listening carefully to what the other person is saying, noticing the words he or she emphasises and using one or two of them in your own speech in a confirmatory way. This gives the person assurance that he or she is being listened to – and understood. Matching the tone and speed of delivery is also important.

If you want to disengage from a conversation – to end a phone call, for example – try deliberately mismatching your voice. This will give a 'go-away' signal without the person consciously knowing why.

Personal space

In social situations, we unconsciously try to maintain a comfortable 'social' distance between ourselves and others. A closer stance inevitably indicates a more intimate relationship.

Interpersonal relationships

Body language is important in interpersonal relationships. Some people even define the quality of their relationships in terms of body language – by the warmth of a smile, the tenderness of a touch, or the intensity of a kiss. Body language is important at every stage of sexual relationships. People flirt through body language, 'making eyes' at one another, tacitly signalling whether or not an approach is welcome. Happily married couples are better at decoding one another's nonverbal messages than unhappily married couples: in one study, unhappy couples were shown to decode nonverbal messages from total strangers more accurately than from each other. Researchers who study divorce have found that unhappy couples who display facial expressions of contempt or disgust in one another's presence are heading for marital breakdown.

Just as body movement is synchronised with speech, so too is it synchronised with the movements of others. Even strangers who are walking along a crowded pavement co-ordinate their movements – if they did not, they would bump into one another. Body language also provides important clues to the nature of relationships between people. Observers can guess the identity of an unseen conversational partner from the body language of one participant alone. Even very young children are able to do this; for example, they can accurately identify whether their mother is conversing with a friend or a stranger. When people get on well together, they tend to imitate each other's postures. Conversely, if someone wants to dissociate themselves from a certain group, or indicate their superior status, they may do so by using dissimilar postures.

Body language can provide important clues to social status. People of superior status tend to be more relaxed, whereas those of inferior status

(F)OCUS ON

PUPIL DILATION

The pupils of the eyes dilate in response to loss of light, but they also dilate under the influence of strong emotion. Star-crossed lovers gazing into one another's eyes may have very enlarged pupils, but so too may someone who is enraged or absolutely terrified. Unlike most forms of body language, we cannot directly control the size of our pupils, so they can be an important source of information about emotion. It is said that Chinese jade dealers would gaze into another's eyes in order to see how keen the other was to close a bargain. In this way, they could secure a good price – unless, of course, they were bargaining at dusk, when the fading light could lead them to some mistaken conclusions!

tend to be more tense in the presence of their superiors. In the context of a group, the most important person is often the one who is looked to or at by other group members. Gaze may also be used by a person of superior status as a means of exerting influence on other people – for example, by displaying approval or disapproval.

Practical applications

Interpersonal communication can now be taught, learned and improved through what is known as communication skills training.

This typically includes instruction in body language. Such training has been used in many different contexts: as a form of occupational training (with groups such as teachers, doctors, nurses and police officers); in employment interviews; as a therapy for psychiatric patients; and for improving inter-cultural communication. For example, some cultures prefer to converse at close distances, whereas others prefer to keep greater distances between themselves – they are literally 'stand-offish'. Communication between members of different cultures can be difficult if people are unaware of these preferences: there are stories of international gatherings where people virtually chase one another round the room trying to establish a comfortable conversational distance. Training in inter-cultural communication seeks to increase awareness of such differences, and to encourage 'mindfulness' when interacting with people of different nationalities.

However, the practical significance of studying body language goes well beyond such formal instruction. Even reading a short article like this may be influential. By highlighting the fine details of social interaction, it becomes much easier for people to be conscious of and change their behaviour, if they so desire. By heightening awareness of the importance of body language, people may change the way they think about communication. We may not always be conscious of our body language or the clues that we receive from other people's, but it is all around us and its significance is there for those who have the eyes to see it.

Social standing Body language can reveal status within a social hierarchy. Here, the relatively tense stance of the more junior worker on the left contrasts with the typically relaxed posture of her more senior colleague.

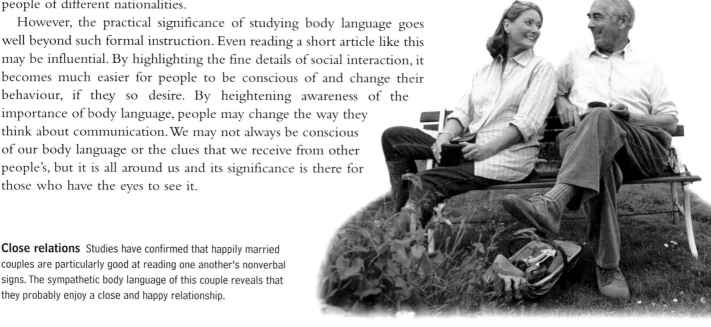

Close relations Studies have confirmed that happily married couples are particularly good at reading one another's nonverbal signs. The sympathetic body language of this couple reveals that they probably enjoy a close and happy relationship.

We often feel more confident in 'reading' people's body language than perhaps we should – deception, in particular, is often surprisingly hard to detect.

HOW TO USE BODY LANGUAGE

However, there is no denying that becoming more conscious of the gestures and facial expressions we unconsciously display can improve how we communicate. We can monitor and refine our own nonverbal signals, and become more sensitive to those of others. The examples below illustrate some of the first areas to look at to improve your nonverbal communication skills.

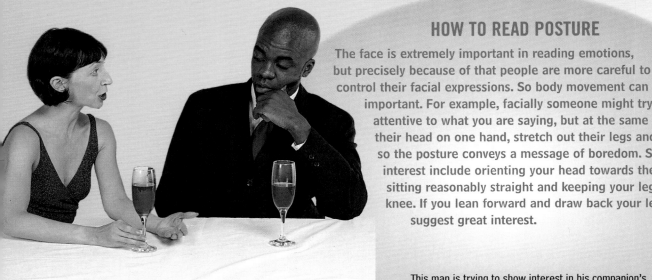

HOW TO READ POSTURE

The face is extremely important in reading emotions, but precisely because of that people are more careful to control their facial expressions. So body movement can also be important. For example, facially someone might try to be attentive to what you are saying, but at the same time support their head on one hand, stretch out their legs and lean back – so the posture conveys a message of boredom. Signs that signal interest include orienting your head towards the other person, sitting reasonably straight and keeping your legs bent at the knee. If you lean forward and draw back your legs, this can suggest great interest.

This man is trying to show interest in his companion's conversation – but his almost sleepy posture reveals that he is actually rather bored.

HOW TO FLIRT

'Giving someone the eye' is all about signalling sexual interest and sexual availability, but timing is everything! The gaze has to be long enough to be perceptible to the other person, but not so long that it seems like an aggressive stare. Repeating the process a few times may do the trick. If the other person keeps avoiding your gaze, you are probably wasting your time, but if the eyes meet and the facial expression shows interest, you may be on your way. For the really shy and reticent, a big smile may also be needed to win them over.

Here the sunglasses are used as a prop to help convey the message – 'I'm interested in you'.

HOW TO MAKE SOMEONE FEEL COMFORTABLE

There are lots of ways of making someone feel comfortable, and body language certainly plays its role. Undoubtedly, bodily relaxation matters. If you are tense, nervous or fidgety, this will make others feel uncomfortable. One useful nonverbal sign that people are getting along is that they tend to imitate each other's postures. See if you can notice how often this occurs in conversation. Try to resist imitating someone else's postures, and you may start to feel you are being really unfriendly! If you wish to create a more positive atmosphere, try to imitate someone's postures (although not too blatantly) – this shows interest and responsiveness to the other person.

The rapport between these two women is clear from the similarity of their postures and gestures.

HOW TO READ FACIAL EXPRESSIONS

Facial expressions can be either posed or spontaneous. So how can we tell the difference? Most revealing is the smile. In a posed smile, often just the corners of the mouth are raised; in a genuine smile, smile wrinkles – 'crow's feet' – may appear at the corner of the eyes. A posed smile may be produced almost as if turning on a light switch, whereas the onset and offset of a spontaneous smile may be more gradual.

Another clue to whether an expression is posed or genuine is its degree of symmetry. An asymmetrical expression is one where the expression on one side of a line drawn vertically through the middle of the face does not match that of the other side. Posed expressions tend to be much less symmetrical than spontaneous ones, so you can use this as a clue to help judge whether someone's facial response is largely genuine, or if it has an element of effort.

In a posed smile, the muscles controlling the mouth are under conscious control as they raise the corners into a conventional smiling expression.

In a genuine smile, many more face muscles come into play, producing raised cheeks and wrinkles around the eyes as well as raised mouth corners.

HOW TO DETECT DECEPTION

Detecting deception from body language is much harder than people often think. There is no 'Pinocchio's nose' that automatically tells you when someone is lying. For example, there is a belief that if someone averts their gaze, he or she may be lying; this may be the case, but the person might also be showing respect or simply be feeling shy.

One useful way to discern deception is to look for very brief expressions, which may occur if someone is surprised, startled, or suddenly influenced by a very strong emotion (such as fear, panic or anger). These expressions may be quickly brought under control, but can be very revealing about someone's underlying emotions. If, for example, you mention an unexpected promotion to a colleague, they might make a fleeting expression of surprise – widened eyes, raised eyebrows – before they regain facial composure and offer their congratulations.

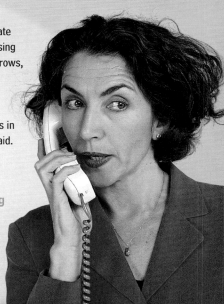

A mixed expression can indicate deception. Here, some surprising news has caused raised eyebrows, which betray the emotions behind the more poised and controlled expression in the rest of the face — and perhaps in contrast with what is being said.

Mind reading

Can one consciousness directly examine another – and if so, how is this done? When we ask questions like these, we enter the realm of mind readers and psychics.

People are endlessly fascinated by mind readers, psychics and clairvoyants. By offering a mixture of insight, prophecy and sheer entertainment, some have built successful careers and have even been sought out as advisers by politicians and leaders. It is undeniable that the best exponents of mind reading are extremely skilful, leaving even hardened sceptics with the impression that they 'know' more than they should. But how is this done?

Cold reading

Many stage mind readers, psychics, astrologers and palm readers, as well as professional salesmen, use 'cold reading' to convince their subjects that they can get inside their minds. This is not a conjuring trick, but a collection of diverse skills – observation, memory and the ability to lead a conversation – that allow the reader to gather surprisingly accurate information about the subject. Proficient cold readers first scrutinise their subject's appearance, speech and demeanour to gain character clues. They build on this initial profile by making 'predictions' that are likely to be true. For example,

Random choice? Stage mind readers know that, of the shapes above, people are most likely to pick the star, especially if this is in second position – so their chance of guessing someone's choice is considerably higher than 1 in 4.

HOW TO BE A 'MIND READER'

Some acts of apparent mind reading are no more than simple deceptions. Here is an example that makes a good party trick. It relies on the complicity of a 'plant', who needs to be secretly briefed beforehand.

First, tell the assembled group that you are about to read their minds. Pass around identical sheets of paper and envelopes. Ask everyone to write down one phrase that is intensely personal to them, and then to place this in the envelope. Collect the envelopes, but be sure to put the plant's entry at the bottom of the pile. Now take the first envelope from the top of the pile and press it against your forehead in a theatrical

way as if you are trying to psychically 'read' the paper inside. Make up any old phrase, and speak it out loud prophetically. This is the plant's cue to shout with amazement 'Those are my words…how could you possibly have known?' Open the envelope and read the words to yourself, as if checking your answer, then discard the paper. You will now have read someone's phrase. Press the next envelope to your forehead as before, and speak the phrase you have read out loud, this time to someone's real amazement. Repeat the sequence until everyone's phrase has been read – or someone cottons on to the trick.

EXTRA-SENSORY EXPERIMENTS

Is it possible to prove the existence of ESP scientifically? In the 1970s, scientists devised an experiment to try just that, and since then the so-called Ganzfeld experiments have been conducted at several reputable institutions.

The idea behind the tests is that by suppressing all normal sensory input (Ganzfeld means 'whole field' in German) the subject becomes more susceptible to picking out the weak signals supposedly involved in ESP. The subject's eyes are covered with semi-opaque material and bathed in red light, while white noise is fed to him or her through headphones. A second person, in another room, then attempts to 'transmit' a visual image from a selection of four, and the subject attempts to identify the image.

In 1994, Daryl Bem and Charles Honorton (of Cornell and Edinburgh universities) analysed the published data from Ganzfeld experiments. On average, they found that subjects identified the right image 35 per cent of the time – a hit rate significantly higher than chance. Many scientists then set about finding flaws in either the experimental technique or the analysis, and in 1999 a rival analysis found that the Ganzfeld tests in fact gave no indication of ESP whatsoever.

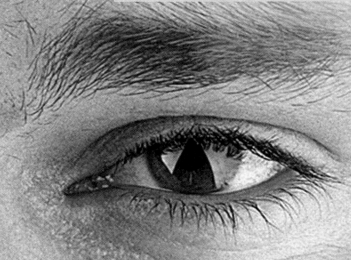

an affluent subject from a cold climate is likely to be planning a holiday in a hot country, so the statement 'I see blue waters and palm trees' is likely to ring true. Responses to such predictions are carefully monitored, allowing the reader to adjust his or her comments and make more accurate predictions, gaining the subject's confidence. This is aided by the fact that people are far more likely to remember correct predictions than incorrect ones, as they seem more significant. In one case study, psychic Peter Hurkos carried out a reading that left a subject stunned by its apparently detailed accuracy. Subsequent viewing of a video recording of the reading, however, showed that Hurkos made 14 incorrect statements for every one that was correct.

Cold readers often exploit our willingness to accept any vague statements about our personality, particularly if they are flattering. This is often called the Barnum effect after the circus showman and trickster P.T. Barnum. In one study, people were so convinced that universally appealing statements such as 'At times you are affable and sociable while at other times you are wary and reserved' were personalised appraisals of themselves that they gave them an average mark of 4.3 out of 5 for accuracy.

Psychic insight?

In a different category are those mind readers who really believe it is possible to reach into another mind through 'psychic' effects such as extra-sensory perception (ESP). But is the skill of such practitioners truly a form of psychic insight – or is it again simply a mix of clever manipulation and mere chance? Studies conducted in the 1950s that 'proved' the existence of ESP have since been exposed as frauds, and much subsequent research in the area has been unreliable, at best. One type of study, the Ganzfeld experiment, has opened up real debate, but the topic remains highly controversial among psychologists.

Seeing the future?
The crystal ball is the classic prop, but fortune tellers are astute judges of their clients' responses, sometimes using touch as well as observation.

CONSCIOUSNESS AND THE DEVELOPING MIND

The brain is a machine that has to build itself. While every newborn baby is born with a set of reflexes, it has to learn how to see, feel and think – that is, how to be conscious – through its interactions with the world.

A baby's brain has to learn how to make sense of its world. Consciousness – in all its sharply focused, meaning-imbued and introspective glory – is not something that we are born with: instead, it is a brain skill that must be mastered in stages.

Learning to be conscious begins in the womb. By 14 weeks, a foetus has a brain. If pricked, stress hormones surge through its body, suggesting that it feels pain. But such responses are just reflexes, as at this age the higher brain is only an unconnected mass of cells. By six months, however, the brain is wired up well enough for the foetus to hear, smell, taste and even blink when bright light shines onto its mother's abdomen. Experiments show that newborns can recognise music and voices that they heard during pregnancy. So significant learning is already taking place in the womb.

> **"Children lose in the order of 20 billion synapses per day between early childhood and adolescence. While this may sound harsh, it is generally a very good thing."**
>
> Lise Eliot, neurobiologist

Brain growth and early experience

After birth the brain really gets going, growing at a phenomenal rate of around a quarter of a million neurons every minute. Its rampant growth is, however, rather random. The connections established between neurons are chaotic, and nerve traffic flows spasmodically across the jumbled

Child's play According to Piaget, there are clear stages in children's mental development. The 'conservation of numbers' stage occurs around the age of six. If counters are arranged in two rows (a), a child sees that each row has the same number. But if one row is then arranged in a cluster (b), a child under six is likely to think that it now contains fewer counters. Older children realise that the quantities must be the same.

a   b

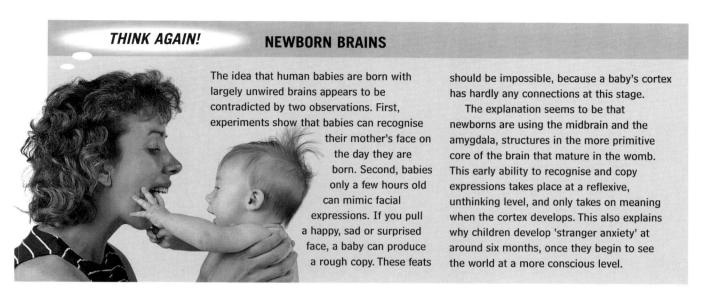

THINK AGAIN!   NEWBORN BRAINS

The idea that human babies are born with largely unwired brains appears to be contradicted by two observations. First, experiments show that babies can recognise their mother's face on the day they are born. Second, babies only a few hours old can mimic facial expressions. If you pull a happy, sad or surprised face, a baby can produce a rough copy. These feats should be impossible, because a baby's cortex has hardly any connections at this stage.

The explanation seems to be that newborns are using the midbrain and the amygdala, structures in the more primitive core of the brain that mature in the womb. This early ability to recognise and copy expressions takes place at a reflexive, unthinking level, and only takes on meaning when the cortex develops. This also explains why children develop 'stranger anxiety' at around six months, once they begin to see the world at a more conscious level.

pathways of the immature brain. And studies suggest that a newborn's experience of the world is very different to our own. In one experiment, babies were shown a number of simple patterns; electrical recordings revealed that their brains took in the information very slowly and responded with much the same surge of neural firing to one pattern as to another. So newborns can certainly see, but what they experience – with the likely exception of the mother's face and breast – is little more than an elusive, shifting shape.

But soon the baby begins to acquire the habits of perception – interpreting information from the senses in a way that makes sense of the world and provides the basis for conscious experience. To carry out this wiring, brain growth actually goes into reverse. Links between neurons are severed and some cells die, pruning back the forest of connections into a more efficient network. The brain discovers through experimentation which are the connections that can deliver focused impressions, and the result is a thinking machine that is shaped to fit its world.

Models of development

There have been many attempts to unravel the thinking processes by which children learn and adapt to the world. The two best-known pioneers in this area are Jean Piaget and Lev Vygotsky.

The Swiss psychologist Jean Piaget (1896–1980) was a sharp observer of children, and he noticed that their cognitive development appeared to follow a natural succession of stages. Just as most children learn to crawl before learning to walk, intellectual development takes place in more or less distinct steps. Piaget stressed the role of the individual child in bringing about his or her own intellectual development. Like miniature scientists, children are always experimenting – banging objects, playing around with them – and gradually developing rules that allow them to understand their world.

Real lives

WOLF CHILDREN

The vital influence of other humans on a child's mental development is shown by the story of Amala and Kamala, two Indian girls raised in the wild by wolves. In 1920, a local missionary rescued the girls, then aged three and five, but he was disappointed by their response. They ran on all fours, ate raw meat, showed no facial expressions and preferred the company of his dogs. Their hearing and eyesight seemed unusually sharp, but they never learnt to speak. It seems their brains had already been formed by their early immersion in a wolf's world, and it was too late to develop the self-awareness that characterises human beings.

Their story had no happy ending. The younger died soon after her rescue while the elder died of typhoid at 16, still more wolf than human in mind.

Some researchers believe that adolescence is a life stage unique to humans – unlike most other primate species, which generally go straight from childhood into adulthood.

Anthropologist Barry Bogin believes that this pattern of development evolved to allow young humans time to master the intricacies of adult social relations. According to Bogin, the fact that boys' and girls' physical development follow somewhat different courses bears this out. Boys become fertile and hormone-driven at about 13, yet their bodies stay puny and

sexually unappealing to females until muscle development in their late teens. Girls grow a womanly shape at puberty, yet are surprisingly infertile until their late teens.

The theory is that girls needed to look like women before they reached sexual maturity so that they would be included in the routine of baby care, allowing them to pick up the essential skills of mothering. Boys needed the sexual drive and aggression of an adult male while still resembling unthreatening children so that they could learn their roles in society without provoking jealousy and violence from elders.

The child begins by establishing some very general expectations about the world. At about eight months, for example, a child will have learned enough to know that when a toy is hidden by a blanket, the toy still lies underneath it. Later the child masters more sophisticated expectations, learning, for example, that matter is conserved. So when a tall, thin glass of water is poured into a short, fat glass, the child knows that the quantity of water is the same in each, despite the different levels of water in the glasses.

The development of a sense of self characterises another important stage. While most children can recognise themselves in a mirror by the time they are two years old, Piaget considered them to be 'egocentric' until the age of five or six. At this age, children begin to realise that other people may see and feel life from quite a different point of view; they also learn that inner psychological events, such as thoughts and imaginings, are distinct from real events in the outside world. The new ability to put themselves in another's shoes in turn strengthens children's own perception of selfhood – they can be objective about their own subjective existence and have more mature emotional reactions and moral judgments.

Piaget's model of development was incredibly ambitious, because it described the complete transition from birth to adult thinking. Many psychologists have challenged the way Piaget reached his conclusions, and have pointed out that he did not try to account for how or why development occurs; nevertheless, Piaget's ideas remain one of the most prominent influences in developmental psychology.

Social theory

The theories of Russian psychologist Lev Vygotsky (1896–1934) place far more stress on the role played by society and language in shaping the minds of children. Vygotsky pointed out that not only are all children born into the same physical world – and so will learn the same sensory and perceptual lessons – but they are also born into well-defined cultural worlds and so their interactions with other people will be a crucial factor in their mental development. Vygotsky showed how children learn to express their thoughts in words, first through talking out loud, then by internalising their speech as a private monologue – a habit of wrestling ideas from the self. Vygotsky argued that many of the things that we consider to be part of our conscious selves are actually the internalisation of socially evolved ways of thinking. So attitudes like loyalty or rebellion, rather than coming from within, are in fact learned from ideas expressed within our cultures.

Lifelong development

Both Piaget and Vygotsky's theories conform to the common-sense idea that babies are born and then develop increasingly complex minds, each new set of mental skills paving the way for further levels of elaboration. But what has recently astonished psychologists is to find that the human brain seems genetically programmed to develop over a prolonged period. Until relatively recently, psychologists assumed that the brain completed its growth and subsequent pruning in the first few years of life, ending with the language centres, which reach maturity at around six or seven. Yet brain scans have shown that the very highest levels of the brain – those that have most to do with planning, social judgement and emotional control – have a sudden surge of growth just before puberty and then are gradually shaped during the teenage years and even early adulthood.

What this appears to mean is that evolution expects us still to be learning important intellectual lessons at this relatively advanced age. The necessary plasticity has been designed in so that we can assimilate a socialised mindset in a gradual, step-by-step, fashion. If the behaviour of an adolescent seems immature (or interestingly experimental, as a teenager would see it), this is because it quite literally is so. The human mind was meant to develop through a prolonged process of adjustment before finally arriving at a state of well-adjusted fit with its environment.

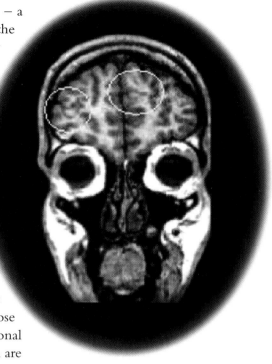

Late development The coloured areas in this image are those in the brain's prefrontal lobes that are specifically active when someone is making a moral judgment. Unlike most brain areas, the prefrontal cortex does not reach maturity until adulthood.

Becoming aware The ability to engage with social and moral issues emerges in the teenage years, as the highest levels of the conscious brain reach maturity.

WHAT IS MATURITY?

In adulthood, we often let our unconscious habits take over our day-to-day life. But there are times – such as when making a difficult decision, or resolving a crisis in our own lives – when we need to fully engage our mature conscious minds.

By the time we reach our late teens, we are in most ways adult. Our bodies are physically mature, and in many respects our thinking skills are at their peak. But at this point most of us will have many years of adult life ahead. So what do the adult years offer in terms of a chance to carry on developing ourselves and our consciousness?

Morality and maturity

Most of us like to think that our ways of judging right and wrong have progressed since we were children, and that developing a realistic yet morally acceptable approach to life is part of becoming a mature, responsible adult. In the 1960s, psychologist Lawrence Kohlberg put forward a theory that is still influential today of how our moral judgment develops. Kohlberg claimed that everyone – irrespective of age or culture – could be placed in one category in a hierarchy of moral development by assessing their response to a hypothetical moral dilemma. At the lowest level was the type of moral reasoning used by children, where right and wrong are judged in relation to whether punishment or reward is the likely result. Next comes the typical adult stage in which 'good behaviour' is determined by what other people, in the social group or society at large, will perceive as such. Finally – and, according to Kohlberg, many adults do not reach this highest stage of moral development – individual conscience becomes the criterion for judgments of right and wrong, and there is an awareness that rules must sometimes be broken for justice to be achieved.

> **"Each individual, to become a mature adult, must develop to a sufficient degree all of the ego qualities, so that a wise Indian, a true gentleman, and a mature peasant share and recognise in one another the final stage of integrity."**
>
> E.H. Erikson, *Childhood and Society*, 1963

FACT FILE   THE CRITERIA OF EMOTIONAL MATURITY

Emotional maturity is associated with the following personality traits:

• Facing reality and dealing with it – tackling problems through finding ways to solve them rather than avoiding them.
• Handling hostility constructively, and looking for a solution to conflict rather than someone to attack.
• Finding as much satisfaction in giving as receiving, and naturally considering the needs of others as well as your own.
• Adapting to change – viewing it as an opportunity rather than a curse and accepting frustration in the short term.

• Being able to learn from experience, and taking responsibility for one's own actions and their consequences.
• Being able to give and receive love, and feeling secure enough to show vulnerability in loving someone.
• Relative freedom from the symptoms of tension and anxiety, such as irritability and pessimism.

Diffusing tension One indicator of emotional maturity is the ability to handle aggression in hostile confrontations.

Early traumas can influence feelings in adulthood – but with maturity, a way ahead can often be found, as 23-year-old Jennifer has discovered.

'When I was little, I was very shy and rather unpopular at school. My mother thought the best way to get me over it was to force me to go to lots of parties, and she persuaded the other mothers to invite me to all the birthday parties even when their children didn't really want me there. Little girls can be very cruel, and these events were just torture – I was never invited to be on anyone's team during games, and the other children used to gang up on me and laugh at me until I cried.

'Nowadays I am very confident and I have lots of friends. I love quiet dinner parties, and going out in a group. But whenever I go to a party and see people laughing I always assume that they are laughing at me, however much I try to tell myself this isn't so.'

Life stages

Many psychologists today see the adult years as a succession of key stages, each relating to life events at different ages. On this approach, there may be no specific point at which maturity is reached. Instead, a different mindset is appropriate at each stage, such as ambition in early adulthood, or pride in one's achievements in late adulthood.

One influential life-stage theory that includes a notion of increasing maturity was formulated by psychologist Erik Erikson. He equated maturity in adulthood with the achievement of 'ego integrity' which is achieved cumulatively, through the resolution of specific crises at key stages during adult life. For example, in middle adulthood the crisis of 'generativity' (continuing creative input into work or family life) versus 'stagnation' (loss of interest in life's activities) occurs. According to Erikson, if the outcome of this crisis is positive – that is, stagnation is avoided – a positive outcome at the next stage (old age) is also more likely. Emotional problems lingering from previous stages – even from childhood – can be resolved at later stages, but often with greater difficulty.

Emotional maturity

In recent years, the notion of emotional maturity has become a popular focus for self-improvement books and articles. But what does it mean to be emotionally mature? An ability to take a considered, constructive approach to life is perhaps key, rather than being propelled helplessly by one's enthusiasms or held back by fear of failure or lack of self-worth. Finding a way to 'live well' in relation to oneself and others – recognising the validity of other people's feelings, and accepting the limitations that our past history inevitably places on us – is also important.

The challenge of happy adjustment to the later years of life certainly requires such an approach. Midlife is a point when we become aware of our own mortality and evaluate what we are likely to achieve in our lives as a whole. Bringing our hopes and achievements into line with one another, so that the inevitable frustrations of later years are tempered by a sense of fulfilment, is perhaps the real challenge of maturity.

Maturity in midlife Erikson's theory of life stages suggests that middle-aged people should seek continued active engagement and interest in life. If this is achieved, they are more likely to deal positively with the challenges of later life.

PASSING AWAY

Different philosophies and religions present us with different ideas about death and its spiritual and personal dimensions. In our modern age, while doctors now have precise criteria to decide when death has occurred, there is still debate among medical scientists about exactly what it means to die.

MOVING INTO THE LIGHT

Some people who have been close to death report powerful spiritual experiences. This account from a medical practitioner in Kentucky, USA, is typical of what are called near-death experiences (NDEs).

'I knew that I was dying, and I felt completely passive. Suddenly, I was bathed in a brilliant light, far brighter than the sun. At first, the brightness was painful, shocking, but slowly I began to feel safer. The light became reassuring and comforting and it drew me towards its centre. It radiated peace and joy and I wanted nothing more than to merge with it. Then, somebody – I think it was my mother, who died when I was a child – whispered to me "Go back, you haven't finished what you need to do", and the next thing I was back in the emergency room, slammed back into my body.'

Many people maintain that NDEs offer evidence of an afterlife. However, the strange experiences may have a more mundane neurochemical explanation: as the brain is deprived of oxygen and parts of the cortex 'shut down', the irregular firing of neurons may trigger thoughts, sensations and memories. The rush of endorphins produced in response to the stress of the situation may explain the reported feelings of calm and understanding.

The dividing line between life and death would seem to be clear. When someone dies, it means they are no longer an active physical and mental presence. But in reality, the boundary does not seem to be quite so sharp, either in medical terms or in terms of our personal experience.

Most familiarly, perhaps, an individual's identity does not cease to exist when they are no longer around to interact with us. Physical absence often makes little difference to our consciousness of a person. Anyone who has lived through the death of someone they are close to knows that the person's identity lives on vividly in the minds of everyone who knew them. We retain an image of the person as they existed most characteristically in their relations to us. If the person was debilitated by illness or old age, this process of constructing them in memory may begin long before death, as well as extending after it. We prefer to think of the person when they were closer to their prime, rather than in pain and reduced by illness. After the person's death or departure from active life, we are still able to perceive how they would have felt and reacted in certain situations, to imagine their thoughts, to hold conversations with them in our minds and to experience them strongly as a continued presence in our lives.

This is not just something that happens when someone dies. We all at times find ourselves imagining how our best friend, close relative or partner would characteristically respond in a given situation, when they are not currently with us. We carry their existence in our consciousness whether they are alive or dead. Thus we live on in the consciousness of others, as we live in theirs and they in ours in normal life. This is the one sense in which we all can experience a kind of immortality – as a force influencing and affecting those we knew in life.

Medical and legal death

The boundary between life and death in medical and legal terms is also not as clear as one might at first think. Historically, medical science had little difficulty defining death – it was the absence of breathing and heartbeat; when these vital systems closed down irreversibly, so did all the other functions of the body. The patient was dead, with the predictable consequence of physical disintegration to follow.

Today, these old certainties have been obscured by advances in medical technology. Doctors can now keep some body systems functioning long after others have ceased. Bypass machines and respirators can carry out the functions of the heart and lungs in patients who have suffered devastating neurological damage and who will never recover consciousness. In effect, the body can be kept biologically alive – growing, developing, repairing its worn-out cells – although it is capable of existing only at a vegetative level.

The rapid development of intensive care medicine over the past few decades has triggered a complex debate about the nature of death. Not surprisingly, this has been led by the medical and legal professions, which demand definition of death consistent with modern practice, and workable criteria by which to pronounce the end of life. This has legal implications; for example, in determining whether an assault becomes homicide.

Defining death

The move towards drawing up a new definition of death came in 1968 when a committee of distinguished US physicians, theologians, lawyers and philosophers assembled at Harvard Medical School. They concluded that death should be redefined as the irreversible loss of function of the whole brain. A person was to be regarded as legally dead when his or her brain was no longer alive and could not be brought back to life. The so-called Harvard criteria based on this definition were quickly adopted by the medical and legal establishments, and now appear on the statutes of all states in the USA, and in more or less similar form around the world.

The widespread acceptance of the new definition of death owes much to one very practical pressure – the development of transplant medicine. Kidneys were the first organs to be successfully transplanted from one

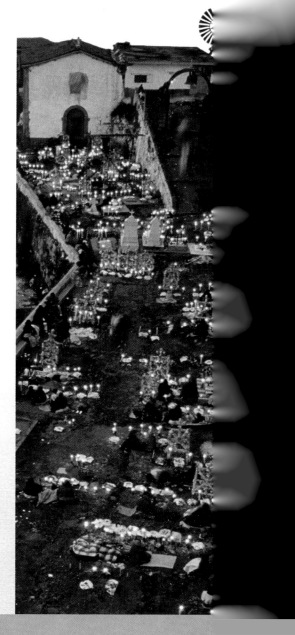

Celebrating with the dead The Mexican 'Day of the Dead' (1 and 2 November) is a colourful and lively festival. Families gather in graveyards to greet the souls of departed family members. They decorate the tombs with candles, flowers, and gifts of favourite foods such as sweets and cakes, often shaped into skulls, skeletons and coffins. Toys and balloons are brought to the graves of children.

THINK AGAIN!   DEATH IN OTHER CULTURES

While we are accustomed to thinking of death as a clear boundary, this boundary varies surprisingly between different societies. In some cultures, people believe that corpses contain a vital principle long after Western doctors would declare death. For example, Tibetans have a tradition of chanting *The Tibetan Book of the Dead* for 49 days when a person dies – this is believed to be the length of time between death and rebirth in reincarnated form. They chant to the body and its listening spirit for a week after respiration has stopped, and then continue by a picture of the deceased after the body has been disposed of.

In Islamic belief, death is considered to be the separation of the soul from the body; and because the soul resides in every part of the body a person may be 'alive' even after brain death has been diagnosed. Further back in history, Jewish people at the time of Christ believed that the soul remained in the body until the third day after death (counting the day of death as the first day) – hence the significance of Jesus being resurrected 'on the third day': any sooner and he would not have been regarded as truly dead.

Many societies invest faith in the continued presence of the dead as members of the social order, with rights and obligations. Conversely, some cultures treat some of the living as if they were dead – for example, if they suffer from a particular disease or have ignored a crucial social taboo. Clearly, death has a social as well as medical dimension – you are dead when your society deems you to be so.

122

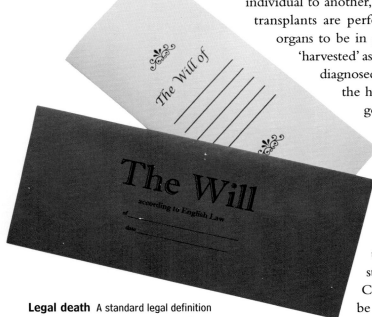

individual to another, but today heart, liver, pancreas and heart-and-lung transplants are performed routinely. Transplant surgery requires the organs to be in good condition, which means that they should be 'harvested' as soon as possible after death. If brain death has been diagnosed, there is no obstacle to the removal of organs while the heart is still beating. Much of today's transplant surgery – and its ability to prolong and improve the life of thousands of patients – would not be possible without the brain death standard.

Between life and death

One of the purposes of the Harvard criteria is to distance doctors from the ethical minefield that now surrounds a diagnosis of death. But there are two conditions – coma and persistent vegetative state (PVS) – that still cloud the issue for clinicians. Coma is a profound state of unconsciousness. It may be caused by a head injury, or a period of oxygen deprivation caused by, for example, a heart attack, smoke inhalation or near drowning. The affected person is alive, but cannot be roused from an apparent 'sleep-like' state and is unable to respond to external stimuli. Recovered patients often report that they were able to see, hear and understand while in the state of coma, which suggests a level of consciousness. However, they had no way of communicating this awareness to other people.

PVS, which sometimes follows coma, is a condition in which the patient loses function of the cerebral cortex – the part of the brain that controls the 'higher' brain activities including perception and conscious thought. However, the brainstem continues to function, maintaining activities such as breathing and heartbeat. The patient may laugh, cry out or make spontaneous movements, and the eyes may even be able to track a moving object.

Legal death A standard legal definition of death is essential in determining, for example, when a will should be executed or when life insurance should be paid.

FOCUS ON DIAGNOSING BRAIN DEATH

The following criteria must all be met before a doctor can diagnose brain death:

- The patient is unable to take a single breath unaided.
- The pupils of the patient's eyes are fixed open.
- The patient does not respond in any way to painful stimulation, such as a needle prick.
- There is no muscle tone in the arms and legs.
- There are no signs of activity in the brainstem, indicated by the following factors:
- The eyeballs are fixed in their sockets.
- There is no cough or gag reflex when the back of the throat is stimulated.

- There is no corneal reflex – that is, the patient does not move when the surface of the eyeball is stroked.
- There is no response when ice-cold water is poured into the ear (if the person is alive, the person's eyes will move).

After these criteria have been checked, brain death will only be confirmed when the doctor is sure that the patient has not taken opiate or barbiturate drugs within the last 24 hours. In addition, scans must be carried out to confirm that no blood is penetrating into the brain, or EEG measurements made to show no sign of detectable electrical activity in the brain.

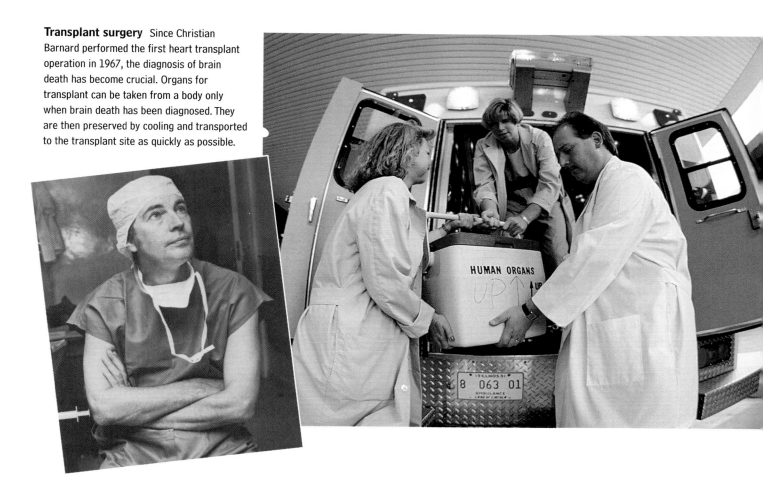

Transplant surgery Since Christian Barnard performed the first heart transplant operation in 1967, the diagnosis of brain death has become crucial. Organs for transplant can be taken from a body only when brain death has been diagnosed. They are then preserved by cooling and transported to the transplant site as quickly as possible.

With intensive physical therapy and medical care, most patients will come out of a coma within four weeks. Many make a full recovery, but some emerge with a range of physical or psychological difficulties. These depend on the severity of the damage to the patient's brain tissue. The prognosis for PVS is far worse. A patient in PVS for more than one month is extremely unlikely ever to regain consciousness, and the few patients who have regained awareness have been severely mentally disabled, blind, deaf or paralysed.

The dilemma raised by PVS is this. Medical science makes it possible to maintain patients in PVS not just for weeks, but for decades. The medical bill for one patient can run into hundreds of thousands of dollars, and today, there are an estimated 14,000 patients in the USA in PVS. Patients in PVS are clearly not dead by current definitions, and yet their prospects for recovery after a few months are negligible. In these cases, should the boundaries of death be widened to include irreversible PVS, and if so, what criteria should be used if we decide to stop feeding and treating patients in this condition?

The matter is still highly controversial, but it is likely that what will follow is a further redefinition of death based on irreversible loss of consciousness — the single characteristic that is most specifically human.

> **"At my age I do what Mark Twain did. I get my daily paper, look at the obituaries page and if I'm not there I carry on as usual."**
>
> Patrick Moore

Consciousness and the soul

The notion of a soul is as old as human civilisation. Its ubiquity across different cultures suggests a powerful desire in the human mind to express the mysteries of life and death, and a yearning to find a basis for immortality.

Beliefs about the soul and immortality reflect the cultures and preoccupations of the societies in which they emerged. Like many potent ideas, they have evolved to maintain their relevance in a changing world. Few scientists today accept the idea of the soul as a separate entity. However, for many people it remains a valuable concept and a cornerstone of religious belief. Even for those who are not religious, the soul provides a metaphor for our conscious and unconscious selves, representing that part of us in which our personality, emotions and free will reside.

Ideas about the soul exist in all the major religions. In Australian Aboriginal and Native American cultures, it was believed that an individual possessed many souls, each of which had its own attributes. For example, the 'life soul' animated the body and departed on death, while the 'free soul' could leave the body during dreams or trances, assuming the form of an animal. If this animal failed to return to the soul's 'owner', the person would die. Similar stories are found in European folklore, where souls are depicted as mice that slip from the mouths of the dead (a red mouse if they have lived a good life, black if not).

The soul in earlier cultures

Many ancient societies believed in an afterlife in which the soul is judged. Such beliefs were held by the Zoroastrians of Persia around 2500 years ago, but were most elaborately developed in ancient Egypt, culminating in their *Book of the Dead*.

The idea of the soul taking on animal form appears in many cultures, reinforcing a common belief in a unitary life force that animates humans and other creatures. Thus, the soul of a Siberian

THE EGYPTIAN CULT OF THE DEAD

The ancient Egyptians held that on death, the soul left the body and entered the underworld – the land of the dead. Here the soul embarked on a perilous journey in search of the god Osiris, who sat in the Hall of Judgement with his retinue of 42 judges. The soul was brought before the judges and the heart of the deceased was weighed in a scale against the feather of Ma'at, goddess of justice. If the heart and feather were in perfect balance, the soul of the deceased merged with Osiris, attaining divine status while retaining an individual human personality. Egyptians believed that the soul was able to return to the world of the living in the form of the *ba,* a human-headed falcon endowed with the individuality of the deceased.

The medieval soul This illustration from a 12th-century manuscript of a text by Hildegard von Bingen depicts the destiny of the Christian soul after death. The person's soul leaves the body, whereupon ranked masses of angels and devils struggle for possession of it.

shaman (holy man) could ride to the spirit world on the back of a reindeer, while in medieval Christian thought, the eagle symbolised a spirit rising to heaven. For the ancient Greeks, the soul left the body on death in the form of a butterfly, which was equated with the breath of life, while in central Asia bodies were fed to dogs to speed their passage to the afterlife.

Chinese myth from the 5th century BC also recognised multiple souls. The *hun* was the spirit of man's vital force, expressed in intelligence and power of breathing, whereas *p'o* was the spirit of man's physical nature expressed in bodily movements. If properly nurtured, these twin souls could attain immortality. On death, rituals were carried out to call the *hun* back into the body so that it did not roam aimlessly but could be nurtured by funerary offerings.

Christian beliefs – in which the soul is a spiritual, immortal entity trapped within a 'lower' physical body – owe much to ancient Egyptian and Greek ideas, especially those of the Greek philosopher Plato (427–347 BC). Plato believed that all higher thought, learning and properties such as virtue belonged to the immortal soul. On death, the soul left the body and entered another person or animal before finally reaching the pure state where it could go on to a higher existence. Platonic ideas of the soul were married with the teachings of the Old Testament and became part of Christian orthodoxy, fiercely protected by a powerful church. It was many centuries before the Christian view of soul and body as separate entities was questioned by the philosophers and scientists of the modern age.

FACT: The word 'psychology' literally means the study of the soul. It takes its name from Psyche – in Greek mythology a beautiful woman who personified the soul and achieved immortality through her love for the god Eros.

5 AWARENESS AND CREATIVITY

We all like to feel and perform at our best – and being alert and 'in the moment' is very much a part of that. While some people seem to have a natural talent for living each moment to the full, most of us need a helpful nudge to remind us not to worry or be distracted unnecessarily. However, there are techniques that can help anyone to achieve a more focused, more conscious awareness in everyday life.

Some of these techniques have come out of what psychologists have discovered about how the human mind processes information – both the limits of our capacity and the conditions under which our minds operate best. Others are based on mind training techniques, such as meditation and mindfulness, derived from Eastern religions, particularly Buddhism. These methods may take a while to master, but the benefits they bring can be profound.

As many who have practised some of these techniques will testify, a heightened awareness can enhance life in countless ways. But perhaps the most satisfying outcome of a fully active consciousness is being able to express ourselves creatively in whatever field of endeavour interests us most.

ACTIVE CONSCIOUSNESS

Being fully conscious means more than just being awake. Engaging your mind fully in whatever you are doing is essential if you are to get the most from each day. You only live your life once, so make sure you're fully 'there' while you're living it.

Many of us live our lives without being as mentally alert as we could be. Instead of being fully engaged in what we are doing, we tend to be easily distracted by those things that catch our attention – whether from the outside environment or from our own passing thoughts. As a result, we may fail to get the most from our experiences.

Modern pressures of living are partly to blame for this. Many of us lead ever-busier lives during which we are expected to juggle multiple responsibilities. Consequently, our minds are pulled away from what we are engaged in towards everyday anxieties and distractions. You can see this for yourself if you close your eyes for one minute, and review the thoughts that run through your head. You will probably find that one thought leads to another, and then another, taking you away from your original point of focus. Memories, ideas, hopes, anxieties, frustrations and reminders of things you mustn't forget to do may all have surfaced during the minute, perhaps with their attendant emotions. Try to gauge how many different thoughts you had during the minute. Multiply this number by 960 – the number of minutes in an average waking day – and you'll get some idea of the extent to which our haphazard thinking impinges on our lives.

Memory and consciousness

We may sometimes be confronted by the lack of awareness of what is going on in our minds. Some mistakes reveal all too clearly our diminished ability to make mental connections because our minds have become over-compartmentalised. Consider this example: Philip arranges to meet a friend for lunch on the following Wednesday; the next day, he agrees to chair a lunchtime meeting at work on the same Wednesday. He holds both of these appointments in mind – but fails to realise that they are incompatible, until too late. You may have had a similar experience, where one part of your consciousness seems to be strangely cut off from another. How can this happen when we are seemingly awake and aware?

It is tempting to put such lapses down to poor memory. And as we get older, the amount we can hold actively in memory may indeed diminish. But in a case like this, where we remember both events and simply fail to bring them together in

HOW TO.... ?

IMPROVE ACTIVE CONSCIOUSNESS
Have you ever been frustrated by your inability to remember the details of a film or book just a short time after seeing or reading it? A simple solution is to keep notes in a journal. When you finish a book, take 20 minutes to sketch the plot and main characters, and record your feelings about the book. Knowing that you will be doing this will help to keep your attention more engaged while you are actually reading. Mentally highlight key scenes and events, memorable quotes, and descriptions that trigger a particularly strong response in you.

our minds, it seems that more subtle failure is in operation. The answer, in some sense, is a lack of 'active consciousness', where the various parts of mental life – conscious and unconscious, past and present, personal and professional – are not as open to one another as we would like.

Cultivating active consciousness

So how can we achieve a better level of mental integration? Certainly, our minds seem to have no problem becoming fully engaged when we face novel situations that are charged with danger or opportunity. Some individuals deliberately seek out exhilarating situations or take part in dangerous sports – bungie jumping, racing, sky-diving – in order to feel 'wide awake' and 'alive'. But such pursuits do not solve the challenge of maintaining focus and attention in everyday life; this requires a sea change in our way of thinking.

One worthwhile approach is to try to open our minds more to the world we live in. While our lives may revolve around our own material concerns and those of the people closest to us, we can – and perhaps, as fellow human beings, we should – include in our awareness the concerns of those remote from us. Being able to feel emotionally the concerns of those who are not known to us is a rare and great quality, but appreciating these with the mind is something that all civilised people should aspire to and attain. Political or charitable activities are ways to take this further; but even without such practical consequences, a more integrated, rational consciousness will follow from deliberately applying the mind to issues that are beyond its immediate concerns. In addition, there are valuable techniques, such as meditation and mindful contemplation, that aim to enhance awareness of our own inner consciousness. These techniques – some of which are explored in the following pages – can help us to live more in the present moment and less in a tangle of associations, memories and anxieties. They can optimise our mental abilities and enrich our lives with more value and purpose.

> **"The perfect man employs his mind as a mirror; it grasps nothing, it refuses nothing, it receives but does not keep."**
>
> Suzuki Roshi, Zen master

 TRY IT YOURSELF

INCREASING AWARENESS

Try this exercise in becoming more aware of your surroundings. Go for a walk with a companion in a local park that offers a good variety of sights and activities. Afterwards, each of you write a list of questions to test the the other's alertness. For example, what colour were the flowers in the flowerbed by the tea shop? Were there any geese on the pond? Were the boys on the left playing frisbee or football? What different breeds of dog were being walked? What is the statue next to the bridge?

Try to maintain a level of consciousness in everyday life that would enable you to answer similar questions about any experience. For example, when you are next being driven by car on an unfamiliar route, take more notice of the journey. Not only will you find it easier to navigate yourself another time, but you may notice some intriguing local features you would otherwise miss.

THE ALERT MIND

Alertness is a key aspect of consciousness. When we are not alert, we do not function at the peak of our mental ability. Maximising alertness therefore helps us to function more efficiently. It can also help us to avoid potentially dangerous errors, for example when driving, working with machines or making vital decisions.

The difference between being very sleepy and feeling wide awake is usually obvious, and we can recognise these extremes of alertness both in ourselves and in other people. Less obvious, however, are the different degrees of alertness that occur throughout a normal day.

Many scientists distinguish between two kinds of alertness – tonic and phasic. Tonic alertness is associated with biological rhythms, especially the daily cycle of waking and sleeping. Typically, our alertness is lowest in the very early hours of the morning (3 to 6 am) and highest during the late afternoon and early evening (4 to 7 pm). We also tend to be more alert during mid-morning (10 am to 1 pm) than in the early afternoon (1 to 3 pm).

> **"I believe the greatest asset a head of state can have is the ability to get a good night's sleep."**
>
> Harold Wilson, former British prime minister

Tonic alertness is controlled largely by a part of the brain called the reticular activating system (RAS), which arouses the rest of the brain when it is itself stimulated. Evidence for this comes from studies that have found that damage to the brainstem above the RAS can cause continuous sleep, whereas damage below the RAS does not impair normal cycles of alertness and sleep. Electrical stimulation of the RAS also causes sleeping animals to wake up. Recent research has demon-

Real lives *A LUCKY ESCAPE*

Jean commutes weekly between London and the north of England. She learned the hard way about the importance of keeping alert while driving.

'We'd had the cottage in the country for a few months, but this was the first time I'd driven back to London on my own. I was a little nervous about finding my way through the country roads, but once I was on the motorway I felt fine. Even though I had only a small city car, I put my foot down and headed south as fast as I could. By the time I was 80 miles or so from London, I had been driving for several hours and knew I was tired, but I felt my destination was within reach and I really wanted to keep going. So I pressed on – and the next thing I knew was when I opened my eyes, with the car drifting into the next lane! I had drifted off to sleep, with the tiredness and monotony of motorway driving. Luckily, it was only for a moment, otherwise I'm sure I would have been killed. Now, I'll pull over to rest as soon as I feel tired or that my attention is drifting. It may take longer to reach your destination – but if you're too tired to drive safely, you're quite likely not to make it at all.'

FOCUS ON   *CHOCOLATE AS A STIMULANT*

Chocolate has been used as a stimulant in many cultures. It was revered by the Aztecs and Maya who used it in religious ceremonies and valued it more highly than gold.

Chocolate is made from the seeds of the tropical cacao tree, *Theobroma cacao*, a name derived from two Greek words: 'theos' meaning gods and 'broma' meaning food. Its active ingredients include caffeine and theobromine, both of which are potentially addictive alkaloid stimulants.

Despite its caffeine content, chocolate does not seem to keep people awake at night and is widely used as a bedtime drink. Theobromine has been proven to improve the performance of racehorses, and feeding racehorses chocolate, cocoa beans or theobromine before a race is now illegal. It has not yet been shown that chocolate improves alertness or other performance criteria in humans – but that does not seem to reduce our appetite for this 'food of the gods'.

strated that other parts of the brain, including the thalamus and hypothalamus, are also involved in the sleep–wake cycle and alertness.

The other kind of alertness, known as phasic alertness, is a short-term, temporary arousal, prompted by new and important events around us, particularly potentially threatening ones. Typically, phasic alertness lasts for just a few seconds. For example, if you suddenly hear a loud noise, you will automatically turn to see where it is coming from. Many other bodily changes are also triggered – dilation of pupils, increase of heart-rate and breathing, tensing of muscles, and so on. These are all part of the response to the potential danger or crisis, and prepare your body either to run away from the threat or to stand and fight it. Accordingly, this mechanism is often called the 'fight-or-flight' response.

The impact of environment

Environmental factors are important in maintaining alertness – a fact often overlooked in the design of offices and factories. Many people work in offices where light, temperature and noise levels are optimised for comfort rather than maximum alertness; indeed many places of employment are more conducive to sleep than work. Sitting in an artificicially controlled atmosphere, while staring at a computer monitor and lulled by the hum of the fans, it is unsurprising that many of us sometimes find it difficult to concentrate.

It is useful to remember that cool, dry air – especially on the face – can help keep you alert, whereas heat and humidity tend to make you drowsy. Therefore, turning down the thermostat and opening windows are all simple, healthy ways to improve alertness. Another tactic to help maintain alertness, particularly during a difficult or boring task, is to take regular short breaks.

Phasic alertness Any sudden loud noise, such as a balloon bursting, makes us jump. This short-term arousal is known as phasic alertness. This mechanism evolved as a means of allowing us to respond quickly to potential threats in the environment.

NAPS IN FLIGHT

Long-haul flight crews regularly experience extended periods of duty while crossing multiple time zones, which results in disruption of daily cycles and loss of sleep. In a recent study, a group of pilots was monitored to examine the effects of napping on board during off-duty periods of flying 747 aircraft, which have a flight crew of three.

Some pilots were encouraged to nap while off-duty, while others were not allowed to sleep at all on the flight deck. Their performance was then compared over a period of 12 days that involved eight flights. Measurements of alertness were made using both subjective techniques, such as log-books and anecdotal reports, and objective measures, such as physiological recording of brain and eye activity. Of those pilots who were allowed naps, nearly all (93 per cent) went to sleep, with the average sleep session lasting about 26 minutes.

The study found that the 'no nap' pilots showed reduced performance, especially on night flights, whereas the 'nap' pilots had significantly better performance and physiological alertness. Partly as a result of this real-life research, many airlines have now put in place programmes for controlled rest periods for their flight crews.

Food and alertness

Food and drink may have a direct bearing on alertness. People often feel sleepy soon after eating a large meal, because of the diversion of blood and oxygen away from the brain to the digestive areas. In addition, certain foods, including bananas, milk, chicken and turkey, promote sleepiness in certain individuals. Conversely, a simple glass of water can make you feel more awake. Many people use caffeine in the form of coffee, tea and cola drinks to boost alertness temporarily. Reliance on caffeine can be counter-productive because the more you use it, the more you need to produce the same effect. On the other hand, some people are so sensitive to caffeine that just one cup of coffee can disrupt their sleep.

In recent years there have been numerous claims that food supplements can reduce fatigue and increase alertness. Compounds and preparations such as acetyl-L-carnitine, DMAE, ginkgo biloba, ginseng, L-phenyl-alanine, L-tyrosine (the last two being amino acids that are commonly found in high-protein foods) have all been touted as substances that enhance alertness. In most cases, these claims have not been substantiated by scientific evidence.

The role of sleep

The single factor that exerts the strongest effect on alertness is sleep. Experts agree that most adults need to sleep for seven to eight hours every night, while children and adolescents need longer. Less than five hours per night over several days can start to cause noticeable mental impairment including loss of alertness during waking hours; less than three hours per night for a week or more can cause serious health problems. In laboratory experiments on animals, continued sleep deprivation has been found to cause death – chiefly through damage to the immune system. It is there-fore essential to develop regular sleep habits that support rather than conflict with the biological clock in our brains.

The 24-hour society

In today's world, many people work shifts that do not fit in with natural patterns of activity. Some people can cope with changing their patterns of wakefulness more easily than others, but it is vital that all shift workers avoid major sleep loss so they can be alert when they need to be. The dangers of shift workers not being alert, especially in the early morning, may have contributed to major industrial accidents such as those at Three Mile Island and Bhopal, and the *Exxon Valdez* running aground. It is also well documented that road traffic accidents are relatively more common in the small hours.

Part of the reason that alertness drops during the night is that darkness increases the concentration of sleep-inducing melatonin in the brain. So one way of maintaining alertness when working shifts is to make sure that the working area is brightly lit. In the USA, some people take melatonin pills (not licensed for use in the UK because of concerns over its safety) to help them to adjust to a new daily rhythm of work, alertness and sleep.

A useful approach to maintaining alertness throughout the working day, whether you are a shift worker or not, is the judicious use of naps. Your potential for alertness is influenced not only by the amount of sleep you had the previous night but also how long you have been awake. So, for someone who has to work in the morning and evening, an afternoon nap will decrease the number of continuous hours of wakefulness and may help to maintain alertness. Care needs to be taken, however, that the nap does not have the adverse effect. If it is too long, the person may find it hard to get to sleep later on. Also, the period immediately after a nap can be characterised by lack of alertness – often referred to as 'sleep inertia'. Generally, though, studies of strategic napping have demonstrated that they can help to maintain performance and alertness.

FACT: Colour has been shown to have an effect on mood and alertness. Yellow has been suggested as the ideal colour to paint a study, because it helps you feel alert and focused without being overstimulated.

? HOW TO...   MEASURE YOUR ALERTNESS

Levels of alertness are measured by psychologists using reaction times. A simple measure of how alert you are can be obtained with the help of a friend and a ruler at least 40cm (15in) long.

1. Ask your friend to hold the rule vertically between thumb and finger at the top of the rule. Position the thumb and finger of your preferred hand at the bottom of the rule about 2–3cm (1in) apart, so neither is touching the rule.

2. Your friend should then drop the rule, without warning. As soon as you see the rule falling, grasp it between your thumb and finger. Use the position of your thumb against the rule's markings to see how far it fell before you caught it.

3. Repeat this several times and take an average of the readings. Then try this test at different times of the day or before and after meals and drinks to gauge how much your reaction times vary.

1

2

HOW TO BE MORE ALERT

There are times when we are less alert than we would like to be. Sometimes these feelings of lethargy can persist, making us feel unfulfilled, and as if we are wasting time. However, there are ways to increase your level of alertness in almost any situation. Here are six simple techniques that you can try.

USE YOUR MUSCLES

Almost any muscle activity will stimulate the nervous system and help to keep you alert. This can involve fine movements of the fingers, hands and feet, or larger movements of the limbs and trunk. Going for a short walk is an excellent way of shaking off lethargy, but if this is not practical, standing up or stretching out your arms or legs can be beneficial.

KNOW YOUR DAILY CYCLE

Throughout the 24-hour cycle of day and night, your body changes rhythmically in temperature, fluid loss, hormonal secretions, and so on. Most people are least alert between midnight and dawn; most alert during late morning; less alert after lunch; and more alert again during late afternoon and early evening. Some people, however, are 'larks' (most alert in the morning) or 'owls' (at their best in the evening).

Try to identify your alertness pattern, and use this to decide what time of day is best to tackle certain tasks. Establishing a regular pattern of behaviour will give your body clock a chance to work for you, rather than having to fight against irregularities.

TOUCH AND COMFORT

Massage has been shown to improve alertness and productivity. In one study, workers in one group were given a 15-minute in-chair back massage, while another group spent the same time relaxing. Afterwards, the massaged group completed a set of maths problems in half the time, and with fewer errors, than the other group. Several multinational companies now provide back massages to executives and assembly line workers alike to help efficiency. You can take advantage of this effect by giving a brief shoulder massage to your partner or a friend, or perhaps even offering the same service to a friendly colleague: with luck, your efforts will be appreciated and reciprocated!

A little discomfort is also an excellent way of keeping you more alert. When you sit down at your desk to write that difficult letter or work on those taxing spreadsheets, don't make yourself too comfortable. Instead, find a chair that is comfortable enough to support you, but for which you need to use some muscle power to maintain your posture.

MAKE LIGHT WORK

When it comes to illumination, work with, rather than against, nature. Make sure you receive plenty of light in the daytime, but exclude light at night: this will help to set your internal body clock correctly. And when at work, turn up the lights, as this will make a real difference to your level of alertness. If possible, use 'daylight' bulbs, as these give out light that matches the wavelengths in natural light.

ACTIVE SOUNDS

A quiet environment, or one where there is continuous low-level noise, can be conducive to sleepiness. Any changes in sound level will tend to increase alertness – which is why many people work better when they can converse from time to time or have music playing in the background. Try experimenting with different types of background music to see what benefits they bring; many people claim that Mozart's violin concertos, especially the third and fourth, are particularly effective in boosting alertness.

FOODS AND AROMAS

There is no 'wonder food' that can boost alertness, but a healthy, balanced diet certainly improves overall performance. Food can be eaten at times that complement your natural body rhythms. For example, taking care to have a light but reasonably nutritious lunch can help to minimise the typical early-afternoon drop in alertness. Proteins can help stimulate the production of some neuro-transmitters, so make sure you have plenty of protein-containing foods in your diet. Fluids are important too: keep yourself well hy-drated by drinking lots of water, as dehydration can affect concentration considerably. Certain aromas, such as citrus and peppermint, have a stimulant effect on some people. Try dotting a few drops of essential oil around your working area to see if if works for you.

ATTENTION AND THE FOCUSED MIND

Many everyday tasks require us to pay close attention and concentrate, and most people would like to be able to do this better. There are methods we can all use to help to maintain attention, in ourselves and others, although psychologists have found that there are limits to how much our minds can take in at once.

Whereas alertness is about how awake or sleepy you are, attention is your ability to focus and concentrate on something. Although attention is a familiar concept, it has in the past been surprisingly difficult to define and research. A century ago, pioneer psychologist William James (see page 102) described attention as 'taking possession by the mind, in clear and vivid form, of one of what seem simultaneously possible objects or trains of thought'. Another early US psychologist, Edward Titchener, carried out experiments on attention and discovered the principle of 'prior entry' – that is, when there is more than one thing impinging on our awareness, our attention tends to be taken up by whichever one occurred first.

Studying attention

In the 1920s, attention disappeared from academic psychology for several decades. The subject was dominated by the behaviourist approach, whereby anything not clearly observable or measurable – including the concepts of attention, consciousness and even the mind itself – was dismissed as not open to scientific study. From the 1950s, however, psychologists moved away from behaviourism and began to regard the mind as an information-processing system. Attention and conscious thought became central topics within this 'cognitive' approach.

One of the most important early studies in cognitive psychology was carried out in 1953 by US psychologist Colin Cherry. He was intrigued by the so-called 'cocktail party effect' –

Keeping the thread
Even in a crowded, noisy room, we can keep track of what one person is saying to us because the unconscious mind can pick out that voice and keep our conscious attention focused on it.

(F)OCUS ON   ATTENTION DEFICIT

Some people often find it difficult to pay attention for long periods. In recent years, extreme cases of this problem have been classified as ADD (attention deficit disorder) or ADHD (attention deficit and hyperactivity disorder). Usually, it is children who are diagnosed with the disorder, but adults may suffer from it as well.

Symptoms of ADHD include both inattentive and impulsive behaviour. Typically, a person affected by the disorder may:

• seem not to listen when spoken to directly
• fail to give close attention to details or make careless mistakes
• have difficulty sustaining attention in tasks or play activities
• become easily distracted by extraneous stimuli
• blurt out answers before questions have been completed
• fidget and show other signs of restlessness
• have difficulty waiting for his or her turn
• interrupt or intrude on others, for example by butting into their conversations or games.

It is not known definitely what causes ADHD, although both biological and psychological factors are thought to be involved, and certain foodstuffs – including caffeine and some common food colourings – are thought by some

to make the symptoms worse. Recent research has found that giving affected children magnesium supplements for six months seemed to improve their symptoms significantly. However, further studies are needed to clarify the specific role of magnesium in ADHD.

how we are able to follow just one conversation when many people are talking at once. Using experiments with headphones, Cherry found that we unconsciously use physical characteristics (for example, the gender of the speaker or the direction of their voice) to pick out one voice from the many we are hearing.

Building on the information-processing idea, psychologist and former engineer Donald Broadbent argued that attention is basically a limited-capacity information channel. The brain receives far more information than it can cope with, so incoming material is 'filtered' to select only a small amount for full attention, largely depending – as Cherry had found – on its physical characteristics. The rest of the information is relegated to a much-reduced level of processing, but is not entirely discarded. This is why, for example, you can immediately 'tune in' if someone says your name in a conversation that you are not actually listening to.

Divided attention

More recent theories of attention have addressed the problem of how we can apply our attention to more than one activity. In the 1990s, researchers argued that there is an important distinction between focused and divided attention. In focused attention, you try to select only one thing to attend to, even though two or more activities are going on around you – perhaps if you have to work somewhere that has distractions. Divided attention, on the other hand, is when you are trying to do two things at once – such as driving a car and carrying on a conversation with your passenger. The researchers found three main factors that affect how successfully tasks are achieved under divided attention. First, the more difficult one or both

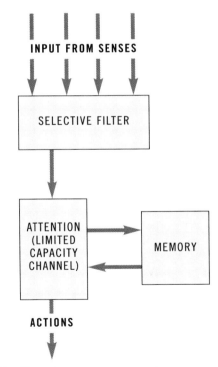

The filter theory As we cannot give our attention to all the information arriving at our senses, Broadbent argued that a 'filter' operates to select which material receives full processing within attention. Once in consciousness, this material can interact with information retrieved from memory.

OPEN TO DISTRACTION

Margaret was 39 years old when she moved from a publishing firm, where she'd had her own office for 15 years, to a dotcom business with open-plan offices. After six months of sharing a large space with 30 other people, she said, 'I just couldn't stand it. My ability to focus went down during the week so by Friday I couldn't concentrate at all.' The noise level was so high that, when she was on the telephone, she would often have to plug her other ear to hear what was being said. Fortunately, the company moved to new premises, where there was enough space for Margaret to screen off an area for herself, and she decided to stay.

tasks are, the less successful dual-performance is. Second, practice reduces the amount of attention a task demands – an experienced driver will find it easier to converse with a passenger than will a learner. The third factor is similarity: tasks that are less similar tend to be easier to perform because they interfere with each other less. For example, a person may be able to converse while driving but find it impossible to hold two conversations or read two things at once.

Distractions at work

Background noise and activity can be very detrimental to our ability to keep our attention focused at work. Since the early 1990s, there has been a trend towards open-plan offices. While some staff may thrive on the buzz of frequent interactions, others suffer because they find it so hard to concentrate. Recent research in the USA shows that open-plan offices can significantly reduce both job satisfaction and productivity. A six-year study involving managers and employees in major organisations such as Lockheed, Sun Microsystems and Microsoft showed that the most important factor in job satisfaction and performance is the ability to concentrate on work without distraction. But, while at least half of all professionals' time is spent doing quiet, focused work, about two-thirds of people in open offices are seriously disturbed by the conversations of other people. Mike Brill, who summarised the research, concluded that offices that have no enclosures are 'ludicrous'.

> "Open-plan offices are big time-wasters. It takes the average person five to ten minutes to get back to a deep level of concentration after being interrupted. Multiply that by ten times a day and you have 50–100 minutes of wasted time."
>
> Martella Keniry, US workplace consultant

However, not everyone agrees that open-plan offices are a bad idea. For example, Gary Horwitz, vice-president of a California-based internet company, maintains that, from his experience, 'the openness of the space is conducive to a free flow of communication and problem-solving'. The solution to these opposing views may well lie in personality: the introverts among us are likely to work better in quieter environments, while extraverts may be better off in noisier, more stimulating places. Perhaps in the future, therefore, staff will be able to request an environment suited to their temperament – for lower stress and higher productivity all round.

HOW TO PAY ATTENTION

Keep the following advice in mind when you are trying to pay attention to a task that demands concentration, such as studying.

• Get yourself into the right frame of mind when preparing to start the task. Remind yourself of the purpose of the task: relate it to specific short-term or long-term goals.

• Decide on a place and time (for example, a one-hour period) when you will study. If necessary, tell people that you do not want to be disturbed. If you are working at home, perhaps unplug the phone or switch on the answerphone.

• Make sure that your environment is conducive to studying. The study area should be well lit, and the temperature should be comfortable but slightly on the cool side. The work surface and surrounding area should be uncluttered, but everything you need should be easily accessible.

• Try to eliminate obtrusive thoughts that will divert your attention. For example, if you have a lot of pressing things to do, write a list prioritising them before you start studying. If any ideas come while you are studying, add them to the list and tell yourself they can be dealt with after the study period.

• If you are intending to study for longer than an hour, take a break for at least ten minutes between periods. Get up for a drink or go outside for some fresh air.

• If you discover any extra concentration strategies that work for you, note them down.

HOW TO HOLD ATTENTION

While many people need to give talks as part of their work, at some time we are all likely to have to address a group of people – perhaps at a family event or an office party. Afterwards we would all like people to say 'That was interesting!'

There are no foolproof rules for being a good speaker, but keeping your audience engaged is a vital component. To do this, you will need to include some attention-grabbing elements. Bear in mind that people respond to novelty, so try to have lots of variety within your talk. For example:

• Liven up the presentation of factual material by telling a story that illustrates your point, or add some action by holding up a prop or moving around the room.

• Add visual interest – write on a flip chart or board, or project a slide with bullet points, diagrams or other pictures.

• Interact directly with the audience. Ask them questions, or encourage them to comment on what you have said.

You can also use examples to hold the attention of the audience and illustrate your points. When using examples in a talk, keep the following points in mind:

• Be clear and make sure your examples clarify the point you are making. If the connection between your point and the example is weak or tangential, you will lose your audience.

• Be relevant. Don't include jokes simply for the sake of getting a few laughs. Your material also has to be relevant.

• Be brief. If you are giving a ten-minute speech, don't use an eight-minute example.

• Target the audience. Keep the specific interests of your audience in mind. For example: if making a presentation to an audience of gardeners, you might tell a story about Alan Titchmarsh; while to a group of entrepreneurs you might use an anecdote about Richard Branson.

• Use personal experience. Using illustrations of things that happened to you helps to hold an audience's attention. Such examples tend to be more vivid and easier to remember (for you and your audience) than abstract or impersonal ones.

CLEARING THE MIND

At any moment, most of us have many concerns occupying our consciousness – present responsibilities, reflections on past events, and so on. A sense of mental chaos can easily be the result. Mind training techniques can provide an effective way of clarifying our thinking, and can guide us through relaxation to inner peace.

"Meditation doesn't teach us anything new. It reminds us what we have forgotten."

Dhiravamsa, *The Way of Non-Attachment*

There are few of us who do not complain about the stresses of modern living. Much of this stress arises because our thoughts and emotions dominate us, keeping us dwelling on the very things that we would rather not think or feel. Stressful thinking is typically unproductive; it solves nothing, tires us out, and leaves us feeling more worried than ever.

One way that we can take more control over our mental and emotional lives is by using mind training techniques, such as meditation. Meditation teaches us that thoughts and emotions are things that we have, rather than who we are. It can free us from the often oppressive influence of thought by letting us acknowledge that thoughts come and go – and it is up to us how much attention we pay to them.

Eastern religions, such as Hinduism and Buddhism, place great emphasis upon meditation. The mind control that it brings puts practitioners in closer touch with their own being, and clarifies their relationship with the reality outside themselves. However, not all proponents and teachers of meditation come from particular spiritual traditions. For example, transcendental meditation (TM), which became very popular in the 1960s, is essentially a secularised technique borrowed from a respected Indian guru. Stripped of its overtly spiritual dimension, TM is widely practised in the US, and even gained government support.

Meditation has also been approached from a strictly secular and scientific standpoint. For example, Herbert Benson of Harvard University Medical School has developed a meditation technique called 'the relaxation response', which has been shown to be effective in reducing anxiety and slowing heart rate and breathing.

THE BENEFITS OF MEDITATION

PHYSICAL RELAXATION Entering a meditative state not only focuses the mind but helps to relax the body.

STRESS REDUCTION Meditation does not eliminate stress, but it does help keep things in perspective.

IMPROVED SLEEP The tranquillity that arises from meditation makes it much easier to get a good night's sleep.

The religious tradition A Buddhist monk in Thailand kneels in meditation by a giant statue of Buddha. Meditation plays a key part in several spiritual traditions.

Meditation for everyone

Anyone can learn to meditate. Many people take up the practice after retirement, or when their children have grown old enough to allow them more freedom. Even the very young can be introduced to meditation. Experiments in the UK have shown the positive effects of meditation in the classroom. Just five minutes of sitting quietly and focusing on breathing at some point in the school day helped children as young as seven to be calmer and more attentive.

Men and women are attracted equally to meditation, and seem to progress at similar rates. Indeed, the main obstacles to successful meditation are not sex or age but impatience and boredom. In the West we have become accustomed to instant results, but meditation demands time and self-discipline. We are also used to a constant diet of entertainment fed to us from outside, and the idea of sitting quietly, doing nothing except experiencing one's own mind, may seem very tame. But the experienced meditator is rarely bored; discovering the serenity and tranquillity of the uncluttered mind gives a unique insight into consciousness itself.

Meditation costs nothing, can be carried out anywhere, requires no apparatus or special clothes, and has many proven physical and psychological benefits, including stress reduction, pain control and even lowering of blood pressure. Meditation is also deeply rewarding as a voyage of self-discovery. Paradoxically, although it is an inward journey, it takes us not away from the world, but more richly and deeply into it.

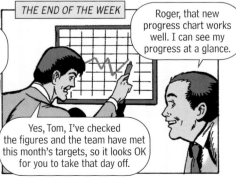

IMPROVED MEMORY Focusing the mind in meditation helps us to become more focused in our daily lives.

GREATER TOLERANCE The mental and emotional discipline of meditation helps in our relationships with others.

GREATER EFFICIENCY Less wayward thinking means that most tasks requiring ordered thinking are performed more effectively.

Regular meditation, even for a few minutes a day, is physically and psychologically rewarding. There are many meditative techniques to choose from, but they all have one crucial element in common – concentration. Not the sort of hard, determined concentration that we used to learn in lessons at school, but a light, relaxed form, in which you choose a point of focus and fix your attention upon it. Every time thoughts or feelings intrude, you gently steer your mind back to this point of focus. Anyone can meditate: all you need is patience and quiet determination.

LEARN TO MEDITATE

STEP 1: GETTING STARTED

Before starting a session of meditation, it is important to prepare properly. Choose a quiet time when you are unlikely to be interrupted. Most people prefer mornings, just after rising, but evenings just before bedtime are also good. Decide what time is best for you and try to stick to it, incorporating it into your daily routine. Choose a place where you feel comfortable and calm; the corner of a bedroom is often ideal. Wear loose, comfortable clothes (or none at all if you prefer). Ideally, you should sit on the floor cross-legged, with a firm cushion that raises your bottom about four inches from the floor. If you find this difficult or uncomfortable, sit in a straight-backed chair with your feet flat on the floor. Place your hands in your lap palms downwards, with the fingers interlocked or with one hand resting on the other. At first, it is helpful to close your eyes, but as you progress you may like to practise with eyes open.

STEP 2: THE PRACTICE

Once you are comfortable, mentally scan your body for muscle tension. Whenever you find an area of tension, gently let it go. Keep your back straight; it may help to imagine your spine as a stack of coins that has to stay balanced. Now focus your attention on your breathing. Make sure that it is coming from as low down as possible – from your diaphragm, not your chest. Don't take huge breaths, just keep your breathing relaxed and natural, in a gentle, quiet rhythm. Now direct your attention to a point just below your nose – the point where you feel cool air as you breathe in and warm air as you breathe out. The sensation is subtle but clear. Keep your attention fixed on this point at all times, even between breaths.

STEP 3: KEEPING FOCUSED

When you start to meditate, you will almost certainly find that thoughts
bubble up and tug you away from your point of focus. Don't try to push them away. Pay them
no special attention; just let them rise and pass across the surface of your mind in the same way that
clouds gently drift across the sky. If a thought does capture your attention and takes you away from your
breathing, bring your focus gently back. If you find it difficult to stay focused, it is sometimes helpful to count
your breaths. Count from one to ten on each out-breath, then back from ten to one again. Another helpful strategy
is to remind yourself 'I have thoughts, but I am not my thoughts'. If emotions arise, treat them in the same way
as thoughts. Tell yourself 'I have anxieties/fears/anger, but I am not my anxieties/fears/anger'. If your
body feels uncomfortable, treat the discomfort in the same way. Observe these distractions and let
them go, instead of becoming caught up in them.

STEP 4: FINDING TIME

Five minutes of meditation a day is a good start for beginners.
As you become more practised, you will be able to stay focused for longer
and longer – perhaps for 20 or 30 minutes. At the end of your meditation, be
grateful for the time that you have spent quietly. Try to get into the habit
of meditating whenever you have nothing pressing to do – while on a
train journey, waiting for a bus, or before the start of a meeting
(this can be particularly helpful because it
calms the nerves).

STEP 5: PERSEVERING

Some people give up meditation after a short time, protesting that their
minds are so busy that they will never succeed at it. But it is precisely because our minds
are so frantically busy that meditation is of such great value. If we were in control of our minds we
would not need to meditate. The key to meditation is quiet perseverance. Even experienced meditators
have 'off' days when they cannot still their mental chatter. Simply note these good and
bad days, and continue with your practice.

MINDFULNESS

Meditation is a highly effective technique for focusing the mind – and for keeping it focused. With patience and practice, it is possible to apply a similar discipline to everyday activities at home and work. The resulting state of 'mindfulness' can improve memory and help us to operate more effectively across a range of situations.

You put your keys down and moments later you cannot remember where they are. You get to the bottom of the page in a book without registering a single word you have read. These scenarios probably sound very familiar. But the reason for these failures of attention – which nearly all of us experience from time to time – is not so much memory loss as mental chaos. Our minds simply wander away, sparked by thoughts or feelings that are at a tangent to what we are engaged in doing. Surprisingly, the more stimulating the activity, the more likely we are to be distracted; studies have shown that college students actually remember more of a lecture they find boring than they do of an interesting one, because the latter sets them thinking instead of attending.

There is, however, a very effective way of training the mind to pay attention – mindfulness. It is similar to meditation, but instead of focusing on breathing you allow your focus to rest upon the things that you are doing, seeing or hearing. Almost like a camera, you turn to each experience without dwelling on the previous one, and without becoming distracted by the inner world of unproductive thinking.

Mindfulness in practice Hollywood actor Richard Gere has been a practitioner of mindfulness since discovering an interest in Buddhism in the late 1970s. He makes a point of meditating daily, saying 'it helps me set my motivation for the day'.

(F)CUS ON MINDFUL ATTENTION

In a well-known psychological experiment, participants are shown a short clip of film without being told the purpose, and then asked to answer specific factual questions relating to the content. What colour was the shirt of one of the actors? What did A say to B? What was on the table? Did C have long or short hair? What could be seen through the window? And so on. Not only do many people get the details wrong, they often disagree vehemently with each other over these details.

One of the reasons for the mistakes and disagreements is selective attention. People tend to focus in on the things in which they are interested and to ignore everything else. With the practice of mindfulness, selective attention broadens, so that the conscious mind takes in more of the information being fed to it by the senses. One outcome of this is that our range of interests also widens and we make better use of our eyes and ears.

The mindful arts
Buddhist monks practising kung fu at the Pagoda Forest near the Shaolin monastery in China's Henan Province. Mindfulness is central to kung fu. It enables the practitioner to focus so intently on his opponent that he counters the latter's attack as soon as it is launched.

Open minds

Mindfulness is not the same as concentration, which demands concerted effort and can only be sustained for relatively short periods. Rather, it involves a natural openness to experience – an openness that we all have as young children, but which we lose in the ever-growing torrent of demands, pressures and distractions.

Practising mindfulness brings many benefits. You will probably be far less tired at the end of the day because chaotic thinking often summons up emotions – anger, fear or anxiety – that are energy-draining and that remain with you long after you have started to think about something else. Mindfulness allows you to let go, and so helps you to conserve emotional energy. But far from discouraging thinking, mindfulness helps you to remain alert, fresh and creative, so when productive thinking is required, ideas typically come with a surprising clarity. This is because the practice of mindfulness gives voice to precisely those unconscious thought processes that are the source of creativity. All too often the conscious mind is too busy with its own affairs to remain open to new creative ideas; and like someone failing to be heard above the noise of the room, the unconscious eventually gives up on its unequal task.

> **"Before I learned to practise mindfulness it was as if I went through each day with my eyes shut."**
>
> Michael, an experienced meditator

There is nothing esoteric or 'way out' about mindfulness. It is simply a way of allowing yourself to remain in the present where you can be fully engaged with your experiences, rather than losing yourself in thoughts about your experiences. Mindfulness is practised by many sports professionals; allowing the mind to wander during a game of tennis, or dwelling too long on the last missed shot can spell disaster. Many sports psychologists acknowledge that the difference between an excellent player and a good one resides more in an ability to remain mindful throughout an arduous match than it does in differences in coordination or athleticism.

THINK AGAIN!

THE SOURCE OF ENLIGHTENMENT

Many years ago, a Japanese Zen master was asked for the secret of enlightenment. In reply, he picked up his brush and wrote the symbol for 'attention'. 'Surely there must be more to it than that?' persisted his questioner. The master picked up his brush again and wrote the symbol three times – attention, attention, attention.

CULTIVATING MINDFULNESS

There are many practical ways in which we can encourage mindfulness to develop. They don't demand any extra time – they are simply different ways of carrying out and thinking about everyday tasks. These exercises will help you to recognise that everything around you is part of a continual process of change. Every time you look at a familiar object you see it in a slightly different way, so in a very real sense everything you see is seen for the first time. Mindfulness helps to open you up to the subtlety of each experience and reminds you that you are fully alive.

STAYING IN THE PRESENT

Avoid constantly judging every event, object and environment; don't let your previous experiences get in the way of the present moment. Thoughts like 'I've always hated this dreary old office', 'I wish I'd bought the larger size', or 'I know this is going to be a bore' drag you out of the present and waste emotional energy. Adopt a similar attitude to people: try to see people as who they are now, rather than in ways you remember from previous encounters. And try not to spend so much time in inconsequential chatter. Watching, listening and paying attention can be far more productive in the long run.

WALKING MINDFULLY

Walking is one of the best exercises for cultivating mindfulness. When you next go for a walk, don't get lost in thought, just look around you. Take in the colour of the houses, the shape of the trees, the smell of the city, the sound of your footsteps, and the faces of passers-by. Notice how your mind tries to pull you away from direct experience by thinking about the things you are observing. Resist the temptation to be distracted until you finish your walk, then think back over the experience. Did you notice things that you usually pass over? You'll probably find that your mindful state made the whole walk much more interesting. Mindfulness makes you far more aware of the enchantment of the senses, how the world arranges itself around us, the difference between natural and man-made objects, and the relationship between objects and the space around them.

TAKING A MIND HOLIDAY

Have you ever returned from a holiday more tired than when you left? Many people find this to be true because their minds become even more distracted and chaotic when in a new environment than when at home.

Next time you go away, allow your mind to take a holiday too. Focus on the sights and sounds around you – the blue sky, the waves on the beach, the green trees and the far hills, the feel of the sun and of the wind and the water on your body, the texture of the ground under your feet. Immerse yourself fully in each moment without letting it pass unnoticed and unappreciated.

STOPPING THE FLOW

Ask a friend, partner or colleague to shout 'stop' at some point in the day when you are engaged in routine tasks. Freeze in whatever position you were in, and pay close attention to all the sensations from the body – tensions, tremors, and especially your sense of balance. This exercise will help you to realise just how much of the sensory material constantly coursing through the brain is screened out in your normal state of consciousness.

COMMENTING ON YOURSELF

Set up a silent running commentary of what you are doing at this moment. Some people are rather dismissive when they hear about this exercise, but it can be very helpful, especially if you lead a frantic life. It will fix your experiences in your mind. Aim to keep the commentary going for at least a few minutes several times a day. For example, 'Now I'm reading this letter ... now I'm putting it down on the window ledge as the phone starts to ring. Now I'm answering the phone and listening ... now replying ... now listening. Now I'm putting the phone down and going over to make some coffee'. Later, when you are trying to recall where you put the letter, the memory will return clearly – it's on the window ledge.

REVIEWING THE DAY

Major spiritual traditions such as Buddhism, which lay far greater importance on mindfulness than we in the West, maintain that a review of the day is of incalculable benefit. In the late evening, think back to waking up that morning, and then go systematically through the events of the day. Focus not just on the events that happened but on your thoughts and feelings about them. Alternatively, go through events in reverse order, working back to the moment of waking. Are there any large gaps in your recall of the day's events? Where was your mind during those gaps – what distracted you? Think about how you can avoid such distractions in the future.

CREATIVITY AND THE OPEN MIND

From early childhood, we are encouraged to be creative – to use our imagination and discover innovative solutions. But can creativity be learned at all, or is it one of nature's gifts bestowed on the lucky few? Psychologists who have examined the nature of the creative process may have some answers.

It is often suggested that you can test creativity, like IQ, using standard exercises – such as listing in three minutes as many uses as you can for a brick, or naming as many things as possible that are both white and edible.

These exercises certainly measure your ability to think of alternatives, but this ability is not quite the same as creativity. A more convincing test would be one that assesses inspiration – your ability to solve problems with sudden flashes of insight. A classic exercise of this genre is the hat-rack problem. You are alone in a room with just two poles and a clamp. How do you make a peg steady enough to hang a hat? Try leaning a pole against the wall and it will slip. Snapping the poles to make legs for a tripod is against the rules. And anyway, the clamp could not secure them. But then – eureka! – you look up at the ceiling and realise that if the two poles are clamped together, to make a single, longer pole, they could be wedged between ceiling and floor, leaving the clamp as the peg. This solution is both surprising and apt – the very essence of creativity.

Out of the blue

Geniuses, who can apparently conjure these sideways leaps of thought from thin air, say that they cannot pinpoint their source of inspiration. Picasso said his paintings took him over, controlling his brush strokes. Mozart claimed that whole symphonies sprang to life in an instant, as if he had just heard them played. Einstein joked that he found shaving risky because this was often the time he was seized by a good idea. All remarked on the contrast between the usual hard graft of intellectual labour and the ease and

"I have no special gift – I am only passionately curious."

Albert Einstein

Real lives   *A LEAP OF INSPIRATION*

The role of sudden inspiration in creative thinking is exemplified by the story of Henri Poincaré, the brilliant 19th-century French mathematician, who solved an important algebraic problem while jumping aboard a bus.

Poincaré had just spent 15 fruitless days at his desk slaving over a problem with Fuschian functions – an aspect of multi-dimensional geometry. Then as he was hopping on a bus, the answer struck. 'The idea came to me, without anything in my former thoughts seeming to have paved the way for it,' wrote Poincaré. 'On my return to Caen, for conscience's sake, I verified the result at my leisure.'

completeness of their moments of sudden inspiration. So what goes on in a brain when it makes such jumps? How distinct is inspiration from ordinary problem-solving? Can we learn to tap into this power? The short answer from psychologists is that creativity increases when we relax our grip on established ways of thinking and free our minds to spot offbeat alternatives. And this kind of mental letting go involves a subtle interplay between the two hemispheres of the brain.

Taking sides

Popular belief has it that the brain is divided into a left hemisphere that is logical, verbal and rational, and a right hemisphere that is emotional and holistic. While there is some truth in this simple model, it is more accurate to say that the left hemisphere is specialised for taking a focused, sequential approach, while the right hemisphere looks at the broader context. Some neuroscientists think that the cells of the right hemisphere are rather more widely branched and connected. So when any thought is in mind, the right side rouses a wealth of associated thoughts, feelings and fringe meanings. When we think, the two hemispheres work in a complementary way. The right brain creates a mental backdrop – a sense of the known terrain – which the focused thinking of the left brain can then explore more systematically.

Of course, the problem comes when we want to break fresh ground. If we are faced with a puzzle, such as making the hat-rack, the right brain establishes a general mental picture – an image of the task, an empty room, a clamp and two poles – then the left brain sets to work logically considering the alternatives. However, if no answer is obvious, if no arrangement of the components seems to fit, we need to let go of our existing picture and find a different context within which to continue the search: the right brain has to relax its grip and start again.

So while intelligence can be seen as exploration within an established mental context, creativity is about broadening or changing the context – letting go and allowing your brain to come at a problem from a new angle.

"The analysis of data will not by itself produce new ideas."

Edward de Bono

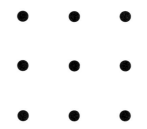

Creative puzzle-solving A good example of a test of creative thinking is the nine-dot puzzle shown above. Can you join all the dots with four straight lines without lifting your pencil from the paper or going over a line twice? See page 159 for the answer.

UNCONCENTRATION

David Gelernter, a cognitive scientist from Yale University, says that the secret of making creative connections is to relax the mind in a special way.

Gelernter outlines two styles of thinking: a high-focus state, where we concentrate on the logical essence of ideas; and a low-focus state, where we think in concrete images, connected by vague emotional associations. Creativity lies in the middle, where the mind is relatively focused, but not on particular thoughts – a state Gelernter calls 'unconcentration'.

To practise unconcentration, take a break from the task at hand to do something not involving active thought. Stare out of the window, do some housework, or go for a walk or a run. Let your ideas simmer undisturbed for a while and you will produce fresh creative thoughts.

FACT: Psychologists have calculated that it takes 10,000 hours of practice to become good enough at something – whether it is chess, maths, tennis, or playing the violin – to master a skill enough to be creative in that domain.

Mental reframing

People who are professionally creative seem to have discovered this fact for themselves. When they realise that they have reached a mental cul-de-sac, they step away from their desks, easels or drawing boards and go for a run, meditate, look out of the window, or go to sleep. By engaging in a different activity, a strongly roused set of ideas can fade and a different perspective may form in its place.

Most of us know from experience that holding a thought or image in mind can suppress alternative views of the same thing. For example, when struggling to remember a name that is 'on the tip of your tongue', a similar but wrong name often rises and blocks correct recall. If you stop and forget about the task, the right name often just pops into mind a few minutes later. This happens because the roused brain cells have relaxed enough to let other, weaker-firing, brain cells on the fringe break through with the correct answer.

Just relaxing from a task at regular intervals is an easy way to boost creativity, and there are more systematic techniques that can also help to reframe a problem (see page 154). But relaxation is not the only component. Creative thinking involves sweat as well as inspiration; the sudden snap of insight can only strike a mind that has prepared itself by forming a rich backdrop of knowledge and skill.

> **"Write down the thoughts of the moment. Those that come unsought for are commonly the most valuable."**
>
> Francis Bacon (1561–1626)

A recipe for genius?

This idea is borne out when we look at the lives of geniuses who claimed that their best ideas came out of the blue. Psychologists have shown that most great achievers started early, and usually had a family background that gave them a flying start in their chosen field. They then spent many years patiently learning their trade.

Mozart's father, for example, was a court musician and composer who was ambitious for his son and had him singing scales and tinkling the keyboard at an age when other children were still on nursery rhymes. By the age of 12, Mozart had already spent five years as a performer travelling around Europe and had written his first compositions. Similarly, Picasso had been taught by his father – an art teacher – to paint with classical virtuosity by the age of 15. And Einstein was encouraged to read the works of Euclid and Kant from an early age. Even after these head starts, Mozart,

The development of genius Creative geniuses usually show a high level of conventional skill before developing innovation. Picasso painted the classical-style *First Communion* (left) in 1896, aged 15. In contrast, *Les Demoiselles D'Avignon* (right) from 1907 demonstrates the bold experimentalism of his maturing style.

Picasso and Einstein took at least ten years before they started to produce original, creative work in their own unique style. They needed to master the complete set of tools of their respective trades before they could begin to experiment within the conventional framework and start producing their unique and innovative work.

As the inventor Thomas Edison famously said: 'Genius is one per cent inspiration and 99 per cent perspiration.' Creative ideas often do strike out of the blue, coming in moments of relaxation or when idly toying with ideas. But behind the ease of the creative flash lies the hard work that is always needed to bring the mind to the brink of inspiration.

FACT FILE   THE FOUR STAGES OF CREATION

British psychologist Graham Wallas has formulated an influential four-stage model of the creative act.

• **Stage 1: preparation** – the intense frontal assault on a problem that familiarises the thinker with all its aspects.

• **Stage 2: incubation** – a period of relaxation that lets established ways of looking at the problem fade so that alternatives can bubble closer to the surface.

• **Stage 3: illumination** – the mental click where some

surprise connection suddenly makes sense of the problem: background thoughts finally break through into clear consciousness, or perhaps we idly note a key aspect – such as the ceiling in the hat-rack problem.

• **Stage 4: verification** – Wallas points out that the click of insight usually produces the feeling of suddenly having the right angle on the problem, but logical left-brain work is then needed to prove that the answer really works.

Creative genius

When Igor Stravinsky premiered 'The Rite of Spring' in 1913, he provoked a riot in the Parisian audience. His audacious music was unlike anything they had heard before. What was behind Stravinsky's creative leap – and can such musical genius ever be fully understood?

In its time, Stravinsky's ballet *The Rite of Spring* (*Le Sacre du Printemps*) was truly shocking because it so blatantly challenged musical orthodoxy. Instead of regular, flowing phrases and smooth key progressions, it juxtaposed uneven fragments in unrelated keys over a barbaric, stamping pulse. Yet despite the booing of the majority of the audience, there were some even on that first night who recognised it as a work of genius.

Stravinsky's raw materials were the same as those available to any other composer – the instruments of the orchestra. What he did was rewrite the rule book, throwing out all the old certainties and profoundly influencing the composers who came after him.

The man and his music
Pictured here in 1958 with the original manuscript of *The Rite of Spring*, Stravinsky (1882–1971) continued to compose innovative and alluring music into the mid-20th century.

The elements of genius

The Rite of Spring was undoubtedly the work of an original thinker. Such creative genius relies on drive and ability, and Stravinsky had plenty of both. He was certainly singularly driven – being compelled to write even in the days following his daughter's death. He also had the self-confidence to face the critics. This was earned, at least in part, through his extensive musical training. The son of a leading bass singer at the Imperial Opera, he was initially a self-taught musician. As a blossoming composer in his twenties, he took lessons with the gifted orchestrator Nikolai Rimsky-Korsakov.

The Rite of Spring represented a creative leap – but Stravinsky had leapt from somewhere: his base was the Romantic and nationalistic music of his time. There are many touches of sumptuous orchestration in *The Rite of Spring,* as well as snatches of folk music from Stravinsky's native Russia. Stravinsky also had the good fortune to live in bourgeois Paris at the beginning of the twentieth century where he mixed with avant-garde artists, including Picasso and Cocteau. Replacing Romantic formalism with new forms of expression, these original thinkers both encouraged and influenced Stravinsky's work.

It is clear that Stravinsky possessed the background, the training, the dedication and the inspiration to write splendid, original music. But do these qualities qualify him as genius – or was there another, mysterious ingredient?

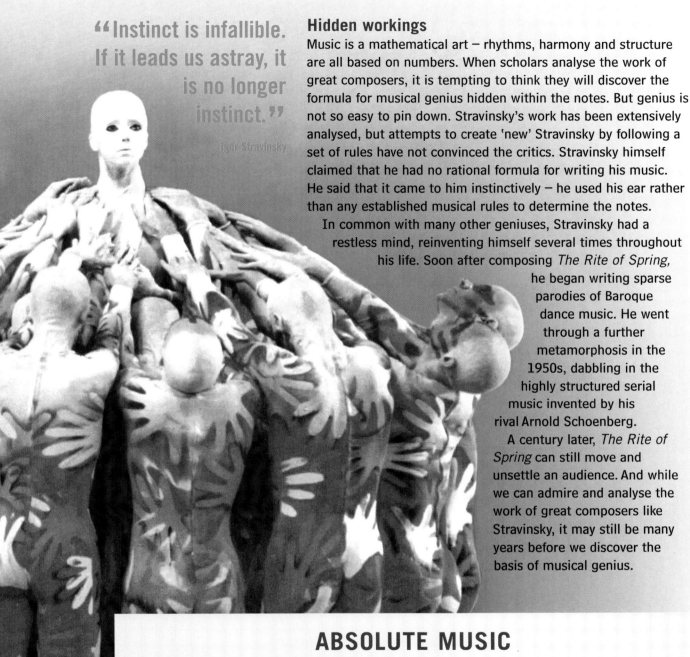

> **"Instinct is infallible. If it leads us astray, it is no longer instinct."**
>
> Igor Stravinsky

Hidden workings

Music is a mathematical art — rhythms, harmony and structure are all based on numbers. When scholars analyse the work of great composers, it is tempting to think they will discover the formula for musical genius hidden within the notes. But genius is not so easy to pin down. Stravinsky's work has been extensively analysed, but attempts to create 'new' Stravinsky by following a set of rules have not convinced the critics. Stravinsky himself claimed that he had no rational formula for writing his music. He said that it came to him instinctively — he used his ear rather than any established musical rules to determine the notes.

In common with many other geniuses, Stravinsky had a restless mind, reinventing himself several times throughout his life. Soon after composing *The Rite of Spring*, he began writing sparse parodies of Baroque dance music. He went through a further metamorphosis in the 1950s, dabbling in the highly structured serial music invented by his rival Arnold Schoenberg.

A century later, *The Rite of Spring* can still move and unsettle an audience. And while we can admire and analyse the work of great composers like Stravinsky, it may still be many years before we discover the basis of musical genius.

ABSOLUTE MUSIC

While some composers work by extemporising — playing with ideas using real instruments — others experiment in their heads. Music that is imagined is free from the constraints imposed by actually playing an instrument, but only the most experienced and gifted musicians are able to work in this way.

Sometimes composers imagine music that is beyond the capability of any human performer. Such work is known as 'absolute music'. Claude Debussy's piano repertoire features impossibly quiet dynamics: in his *Image No 5: And the Moon Descends Over the Temple That Was,* he instructs the pianist to play a chain of nine-note chords that stretch almost six octaves across the keyboard. Chords of this size are difficult to play quietly, but Debussy wants them to start pianissimo (very quietly) then gradually diminuendo (become even softer). And in the early 18th century, JS Bach created absolute music for woodwind: his *Partita for Flute* has long, fast-moving passages without any rests. Players must decide how to break up his imagined, perfect musical line to take a breath.

In the recording studio, however, these limits are removed: today's sound editing technology can make the most challenging piece a reality.

FINDING YOUR OWN CREATIVITY

We all experience occasional bursts of inspiration that give us new insights into old problems. Such creative thinking seems to come naturally to some people, but it is also something that everyone can nurture. The techniques here may not transform us all into artistic geniuses, but they can help to enhance our natural creativity and take us towards successful problem solving at home and at work.

CREATIVE LIVING

- Immerse yourself in your chosen area of creativity, researching or practising as much as possible. Your creativity needs material on which to work.
- Pursue interests in areas well away from your sphere of work and usual occupations. The most creative individuals often have very diverse interests and hobbies.
- Record your dreams, daydreams and doodles. Concepts and feelings arising from the unconscious brain can open up new perspectives.
- Take exercise. Regular exercise increases the amount of nutrients and oxygen available to the brain.
- Experiment with doing routine tasks, such as housework, in completely new ways. Make creative thinking a habit.
- Reward yourself for your creativity, and you will begin to think of yourself as a creative person.

CREATIVE PROBLEM SOLVING

- First, frame the problem. Think of as many ways as you can to express the problem you want to solve, then analyse these to identify the precise question you need to answer.
- Write down any potentially useful thoughts that bear on the question as soon as they arise. Collect them in a notebook and review them regularly to see if they can be applied to any problem in mind.
- Put yourself in a stimulating but comfortable environment, and take regular breaks while thinking about the problem.
- Rhythmic activities, such as walking, swimming, painting, or even washing, can help to tone down conscious thinking and let subliminal ideas emerge from the unconscious.
- Set yourself real targets – for example, a deadline by which a problem must be resolved.
- Get other people to contribute their own ideas. The more ideas you can generate, the better your solution is likely to be.
- Employ creative thinking techniques to generate new ideas – some are described on the opposite page.

MIND MAPPING

If you want to generate creative solutions to complex personal decisions, try this technique derived from mind mapping, as pioneered by Tony Buzan.

• Take a large sheet of paper. In the centre, draw a picture that represents your problem, then use this as the hub to draw out a branching network of associations. Each new thought should be broken down into its components until all possible ideas connected with the central problem are made visible. Hopefully, you will then either spot obvious answers or else gaps where perhaps you need more information.

• Use coloured pens to code different kinds of thoughts – for example, red to highlight drawbacks, yellow to highlight wild possibilities, blue for very obvious connections. Use images rather than words to illustrate your thoughts wherever possible. Go back over the main connections as they start to emerge, making heavy lines that really stand out.

• Once you have made your map, copy it out again in a way that is more organised or that uses some newly discovered idea as the central starting point.

GROUP CREATIVITY

One of the most effective methods of creative problem solving in a group is brainwriting. This technique is often more effective than verbal 'brainstorming' sessions because it avoids social constraints on putting forward ideas to a group, and because more ideas are generated in the given time.

• Begin the session by outlining the problem to be solved. Each participant then writes an idea on a sheet of paper and passes it to the person on his or her left. The recipient can either use this idea as a stimulus for a new idea, which is written on the sheet, or can modify the first idea before passing it on, again to the left.

• After a set period of time, the ideas are organised into groups and evaluated.

RANDOM RESPONSES

If you are simply looking for a new perspective on a problem, abutting incongruous ideas or words can open up new patterns of thought. In the East, this technique has achieved the status of an art form (as in haiku poetry), but it can be adapted into a simple method for triggering creativity.

• Open a dictionary at any page and select a word at random.

• Repeat this procedure until you have a whole list of words, and then apply each to the problem in mind. You will find that almost every word stimulates some ideas on the subject.

• The technique works just as well if you use a phrase as the stimulus: try aphorisms or proverbs like 'a stitch in time saves nine' or 'put the cart before the horse'.

INDEX

FURTHER INFORMATION

BOOKS

Consciousness by Rita Carter
Cassell, 2002
A comprehensive and easy to understand exploration of consciousness in terms of current philosophical theories and the latest scientific research, with contributions from several of the world's leading authorities.

Consciousness by J. Allan Hobson
Scientific American Library, 1999
A learned and often personal exploration of consciousness by a leading psychiatrist, whose particular interests include sleep and the function of dreams.

Consciousness Explained by Daniel Dennett
Little, Brown, 1993
A popular account by an eminent thinker on consciousness, bringing together ideas from neurology, computer science and philosophy.

The Feeling of What Happens by Antonio Damasio
Heinemann, 2000
An expert on the neuroscience of emotions, Antonio Damasio argues that consciousness arose from the development of emotion and our need to map relations between ourself and other people.

Going Inside by John McCrone
Faber & Faber, 1999
Focusing on single moments of consciousness, this book looks at the importance of all the unconscious processing that the brain does before we become aware of something.

The Inner Eye by Nicholas Humphrey
Oxford University Press, 2002
Inspired by a trip to Dian Fossey's gorilla research centre in Rwanda, this book focuses on the philosophical and scientific puzzle of how a human being or animal can know what it is like to be itself.

Introducing Consciousness by David Papineau and Howard Selina
Icon Books, 2000
Comic-book style presentation offering a clear but authoritative introduction to the main philosophical theories of consciousness, and the arguments for and against them.

Kinds of Minds by Daniel Dennett
Phoenix Press, 1997
This introductory book on the philosophy of mind sets out to ask 'what kinds of minds are there' and 'how do we know?'

Learn to Meditate by David Fontana
Duncan Baird Publishers, 1999
A practical introduction to meditation by a master of the art, drawing on Zen and Tibetan Buddhist traditions.

Mapping the Mind by Rita Carter
Phoenix Press, 1998
An acclaimed insight into the workings of the brain, explored using the latest techniques in brain imaging.

The Mind Made Flesh by Nicholas Humphrey
Oxford University Press, 2002
This collection of essays looks at topics including the evolution of consciousness, multiple personality disorder, cave art, religious miracles, and the seductions of dictatorship.

Phantoms in the Brain by V.S. Ramachandran and Sandra Blakeslee
Fourth Estate, 1999
Ramachandran offers insights into the remarkable workings of the mind by showcasing phenomena revealed by people with neurological problems such as blindsight and phantom limb pain.

The Prehistory of the Mind by Steven Mithen
Thames and Hudson, 1996
Mithen offers an original account of the evolution of human consciousness from an archaeological viewpoint.

What's Going on in There by Lise Eliot
Allen Lane, 1999
This accessible book looks at the inner workings of the brains of babies and young children and the evolution of mental skills such as emotion, memory and intelligence.

WEBSITES

www.btinternet.com/~neuronaut
Science writer John McCrone's home page offers a wide variety of articles on consciousness studies for the non-specialist reader. The site provides an overview of current thinking in consciousness as well as featuring specific topics in more detail.

www.consciousness.arizona.edu
This is the website for the University of Arizona's Center for Consciousness Studies. Aimed mainly at academics, it contains details of forthcoming events and offers a wealth of online papers on consciousness-related topics.

www.human-nature.com/nibbs
This is the website of *The Human Nature Daily Review*, which features concise summaries of the latest findings in topics including consciousness, evolution, human behaviour and philosophy, plus more in-depth articles and links to other sites of interest.

www.imprint.co.uk/jcs.html
This is the online location for the *Journal of Consciousness Studies*, a key publication devoted to current research and reviews relating to all areas of consciousness studies.

www.u.arizona.edu/~chalmers/online.html
This is philosopher David Chalmers' home page, containing accessible articles (by Chalmers and others) on consciousness matters. For some light relief, try Chalmers' compendium of philosophy jokes.

PERMISSIONS

The publishers wish to thank the following for their kind permission to reproduce material in this book:
13 extract from *Consciousness Reconsidered* by Owen Flanagan (© Owen Flanagan 1994), MIT Press; **18** extract from *A Writer's Notebook* by W Somerset Maugham, published by William Heinemann, 1949. Reprinted by permisson of The Random House Group Ltd; **28** quote from Alan Turing from the article 'Computer Scientist: Alan Turing' by Paul Gray from 29 March 1999 issue of *Time Magazine*. © 1999 Time Inc. Reprinted by permission; **30** extract from the article 'Is the Brain's Mind a Computer Program?' by John Searle, from January 1990 issue of *Scientific American*. Reprinted by permission of Scientific American Inc; **63** extract from *The Politics of Experience* by R.D. Laing, Penguin Books Ltd, 1967; **72** extract from a letter published in 26 September 1998 issue of *New Scientist*. Reproduced by permission of New Scientist; **90** extract from *Jung and the Story of*

Time by Laurens van der Post, published by The Hogarth Press. Reprinted by permission of The Random House Group Ltd; **92** extract from *Memories, Dreams, Reflections* by C.G. Jung, HarperCollins Publishers Ltd, 1967; **114** extract from *What's Going on in There?* by Lise Eliot, Penguin Books Ltd, 1999; **148** extract from *Albert Einstein: Creator and Rebel* by Banesh Hoffmann and Helen Dukas (© Helen Dukas and Banesh Hoffmann 1972). Used by permission of Dutton, a division of Penguin Putnam; **149** quote from Edward de Bono. For more information on Edward de Bono's seminars and workshops please contact Diane McQuaig at dmcquaig @debono.com or call 001 (416) 488 0008.

Every effort has been made to obtain permission for copyright material. The publishers apologise for any omissions, which are wholly unintentional. They will, if informed, make any necessary corrections in future editions of this book.

ANSWERS TO PUZZLES

DISCOVER YOUR HIDDEN THINKING POWERS:
Page 84 Tease out your hidden knowledge
1: 7 W of the W = 7 wonders of the world
2: 26 L in the A26 = letters in the alphabet
3: 24 H in a D = 24 hours in a day
4: 12 S of the Z = 12 signs of the zodiac
5: 57 HV = 57 Heinz varieties
6: 29 D in F in a LY = 29 days in February in a leap year
7: 2 BOTC = 2 bites of the cherry
8: 10 GB (HOTW) = 10 green bottles (hanging on the wall)
9: 9L of a C = 9 lives of a cat
10: 30 D has S = 30 days has September

CREATIVITY AND THE OPEN MIND:
Page 149 Creative puzzle-solving
The secret of solving this puzzle lies in extending the lines beyond the confines of the 'box' created by the nine dots: many people assume that they should stay within the lines.

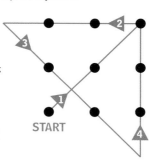

ACKNOWLEDGEMENTS

Throughout these picture credits, the following abbreviations have been used:
t = top; tb = top bottom; c = centre; b = bottom; ba = bottom above; l = left; r = right; ca = centre above; cb = centre below; tl = top left; tc = top centre; tr = top right; bl = bottom left; bc = bottom centre; br = bottom right; blc = bottom left centre; brc = bottom right centre.

6–7 Bruce Coleman/Natural Selection Inc.; 8–9 Bruce Coleman/Natural Selection Inc.; 12tl SPL/Wellcome Department of Cognitive Neurology; 12tr Photographer's Library; 12bl Stone/Tony Hutchings; 12br Photographer's Library; 13 Stone/James Cotier; 15tr SPL/Department of Cognitive Neurology; 15b Bridgeman Art Library/The De Morgan Foundation, London; 16 SPL/Geoff Tompkinson; 17 Stone/Deborah Jaffe; 22 Pictor; 23t SPL; 23b SPL/Gregory Dimijian; 24–5t Robert Harding Picture Library; 24bl, bc, br Warren Photographic/Jane Burton; 25t Frank Lane Picture Agency/Minden Pictures/K. Wothe; 25bl Warren Photographic/Jane Burton; 26–7 Bridgeman Art Library/Vitlycke Museum, Tanum; 26t Bridgeman Art Library/Naturhistorisches Museum, Vienna; 26b Natural History Museum, London; 27t Robert Harding Picture Library; 27bl DK Images/Philip Dowell; 27blc Bridgeman Art Library/Musée des Antiquities Nationales, St. Germaine en Laye; 27br British Museum, London; 28–9 Corbis/Bob Rowan/Progressive Images; 28b SPL; 29b SPL/Colin Cuthbert; 30 Stone/Tim Flach; 31 Ronald Grant Archive; 34 Pictor; 35b Photographer's Library; 36 Image Bank/David de Lossy; 37 SPL/Oscar Burriel; 38–9 Bruce Coleman/Natural Selections Inc.; 38b Image Bank/Malcolm Piers; 39b Photographer's Library; 40–1 Corbis/Robert Holmes; 42–3 Image State; 42b Corbis/Ted Streshinsky; 43t Hulton Archive; 43c SPL/Pascal Goetgheluck; 44 Hutchison Library/Sarah Errington; 45t Corbis/Michael S. Yamashita; 45bl Image State; 45br Pictor; 47 Pictor; 48–9 FPG/Laurance B. Aiuppy; 48b FPG/Peter Lilja; 49c Warren Photographic/Jane Burton; 50b Flowers and Foliage; 52 courtesy of Osborne and Little; 53 Image Bank/Britt J. Erlanson-Messens; 54 Pictor; 55 AKG, London; 57 Moviestore Collection; 61tl Bridgeman Art Library/Phillips, The International Fine Art Auctioneers, London; 61tr Bridgeman Art Library/Museum of Fine Arts, Houston; 61b courtesy of Orion Publishing; 62 Camera Press/Colin Davey; 63 SPL/Gregory Macnicol; 64cl, cr Mary Evans Picture Library; 65tl Corbis/Bettmann; 65b Moviestore Collection; 69t Mary Evans Picture Library; 70 Photographer's Library; 71t Corbis/Owen Frank; 71b SPL/NASA; 73 Corbis/Phil Schemeister; 75 courtesy of Marcus Raichle; 78bl, br Advertising Archives; 79 AP Photo; 81bl SPL; 82b Ronald Grant Archive; 86c, b Hulton Archive; 89t Corbis Stockmarket/Denis Scott; 89b Mary Evans Picture Library; 90–1 Art Archive/Musée Guimet, Paris/Dagli Orti; 90 SPL/National Library of Medicine; 92 Ronald Grant Archive; 93t courtesy of Northern Territories Tourist Commission; 93b Hulton Archive; 94 Ronald Grant Archive; 95t Tate Gallery, London/©Salvador Dali, Gala-Salvador Dali Foundation, DACS, London 2001; 95b Camera Press/G. Botti/Valentin; 96–7 Stone/Tim Brown; 98–9 Stone/Tim Brown; 98b Image Bank/Daniel E. Arsenault Photography Inc.; 99t Image Bank/Ghislain and Marie David de Lossy; 99b Robert Harding Picture Library; 102–3b Pictor; 103t AKG, London; 105 Moviestore Collection; 106l, t, ba Photographer's Library; 106tb Bubbles/Peter Sylent; 106b Bubbles/Jacqui Furrow; 107 Ronald Grant Archive; 108 Magnum/Thomas Hoepker; 109t Photographer's Library; 109b FPG/David Lees; 113 Corbis Stockmarket/C+B Productions; 115 Bubbles/Loisjoy Thurston; 116 Photographer's Library; 117t courtesy of the Functional Neuroimaging Group, Department of Neurology, Professor Arno Villringer and Department of Law, Professor Hans-Peter Schwintowski, Humboldt University, Berlin; 117b Magnum/Martine Frank; 118 Network Photographers/Jeremy Green; 119t Photographer's Library; 120–1 Bruce Coleman/Natural Selections Inc.; 121 Stone/Michael Townsend; 123l AKG, London; 123r SPL/Custom Medical Stock; 124b Michael Holford; 125 AKG, London/Erich Lessing; 128–9 Corbis/Macduff Everton; 130–1 FPG/Chris Rawlings; 131b Corbis Stockmarket/Chris Collins; 132 FPG/John McGrail; 134b Bruce Coleman/Jorg and Petra Wegner; 135bl, br Pictor; 136b Stone/Timothy Shonnard; 137t Pictor; 138 Photographer's Library; 140t Stone/Thomas Del Brase; 141t Image State; 142–3 Image Bank/Eric Meola; 142r Stone/Anthony Marsland; 144 Rex Features/Camila Morandi; 145t Corbis/Keren Su; 145b Eri Takase; 146 Corbis Stockmarket/Craig Tuttle; 148–9 Hulton Archive; 150 Pictor; 151l AKG, London/©Succession Picasso/DACS 2001; 151r Art Archive/Museum of Modern Art, NY/Album/John Martin/©Succession Picasso/DACS 2001; 152l Performing Arts Library/Ingi; 152r Bridgeman Art Library/Private Collection; 152–3 Performing Arts Library/Linda Rich.

Commissioned photography
Matthew Ward

Main jacket illustration: Ian Atkinson, picture elements courtesy of Photodisc.
Inset head: Jurgen Ziewe

ILLUSTRATORS
Stuart Briers 80
Peter Bull 36, 60, 97
Emma Dodd 46, 51b, 84, 85, 149, 154, 155
Darren Hopes 68, 104, 124
John Richardson 140
Mark Seabrook 1, 2, 10, 32, 66, 100, 126
Paul Williams 40, 51t
Philip Wilson 98
Jurgen Ziewe 58, 82

The Conscious and Unconscious Brain was created for The Reader's Digest Association Limited, London, by Duncan Baird Publishers Limited.

First edition Copyright © 2002
The Reader's Digest Association Limited, 11 Westferry Circus, Canary Wharf, London E14 4HE
www.readersdigest.co.uk

We are committed to both the quality of our products and the service we provide to our customers. We value your comments, so please feel free to contact us on 08705 113366, or by email at cust_service@readersdigest.co.uk
If you have any comment about the content of our books, you can contact us on gbeditorial@readersdigest.co.uk

Copyright © 2002 Reader's Digest Association Far East Limited
Philippines Copyright © 2002 Reader's Digest Association Far East Limited

Origination: Colour Systems Limited, London
Printing and Binding: Printing Industria Gráfica SA, Barcelona

ISBN 0 276 42645 2
BOOK CODE 620 003–1
CONCEPT CODE UK 0048/G/S